FINDING FORTUNE

Documenting and Imagining the Life of Rose Fortune (1774-1864)

Brenda J. Thompson

SSP
Publications

SSP Publications recognizes the support of the Province of Nova Scotia. We are pleased to work in partnership with the Department of Communities, Culture and Heritage to develop and promote our cultural resources for all Nova Scotians.

NOVA SCOTIA

Design: Gwen North

Canada 150 Rose Fortune commemorative postage stamp on cover courtesy of Durline Melanson, President of The Historical Association of Annapolis Royal

Library and Archives Canada Cataloguing in Publication

Title: Finding Fortune : documenting and imagining the life of Rose Fortune, 1774-1864 / Brenda J Thompson.

Names: Thompson, Brenda, 1963- author.

Description: Includes bibliographical references and index.

Identifiers: Canadiana 20190084510 | ISBN 9781989347034 (softcover)

Subjects: LCSH: Fortune, Rose, 1774-1864. | LCSH: Fortune, Rose, 1774-1864—Family. | CSH: Black loyalists—Nova Scotia—Annapolis Royal—Biography. | Black Canadian women—Nova Scotia—Annapolis Royal—Biography | LCSH: African American women—Nova Scotia—Annapolis Royal—Biography. | LCSH: Annapolis Royal (N.S.)—Biography. LCG-FT: Biographies.

Classification: LCC FC2349.A55 Z49 2019 | DDC 971.6/33004960092—dc23

eBook ISBN 978-1-989347-04-1

BISAC HIS036030 HIS054000 HIS006010 SOC054000

SSP Publications

Box 2472, Halifax, N.S. B3J 3E4 Canada
www.sspub.ca
sspub@hotmail.com

Printed in Canada

Table of Contents

Dedicated to the memory of Daurene Lewis (1943–2013),
who always wanted to know more about her ancestor.

Foreword

I started researching my family history in the early 2000s. I knew Rose Fortune was my great-great-great grandmother. However, I knew very little about her; she was just another name in the list of names that made up my family tree. In 2010 Ian Lawrence, a genealogist who had been conducting research on different families in Annapolis Royal, contacted my sister to discuss our family history. My mother had worked for his family for over twenty years (1960s to the 1980s) and he had shared a special connection with her. My cousin Rollins had also been researching the family tree and we all agreed to meet with Ian and discuss our research. Rose Fortune's name came up multiple times and we all wanted to learn more about her.

I knew I had come from a long line of strong women. My mother, sisters and I have always conveyed a determination that is not easily shaken, nor dismissed. As a child, I fantasized that I was the descendant of some important figure in history. However, I never imagined that these childhood fantasies would become a reality. The more I learned about Rose Fortune, the more I wanted to know. Who was she? Where did she come from? How did she become not only the first female police officer in Canada but the first Black police officer as well? Who would have thought that the little town of Annapolis Royal was the home of such an important figure in Canadian history? And to add to all this she was MY great-great-great grandmother.

I later contacted Brenda Thompson, a published author, who was interested in writing a book on Rose Fortune. We met multiple times, shared information and I agreed to do a DNA test to confirm my family's historical background. My DNA results were somewhat surprising. I knew my ancestors originated from Africa, however I didn't expect there to be so much diversity within my DNA. My ancestry stretched across Africa, into the

Middle East, throughout Europe, across both North and South America and into the Philippines. I had been told at a young age that some of my ancestors were First Nation and the DNA results confirmed this. However, I was surprised to learn that my First Nation ancestry came from both North and South America. Brenda's research uncovered a "runaway slave" poster looking for Rose's parents, Aminta and Fortune. The poster stated that Rose's mother had "the Look of an Indian, and is so, her Mother having been brought from the Spanish Main to Rhode Island." The DNA tests confirmed my connection to Aminta.

The runaway slave advertisement for Fortune and Aminta was deeply disturbing. I was enraged when I read the ad. Bradley's description of Fortune and Aminta showed no more respect than if he had been searching for a lost barn animal. The dehumanizing terminology described Aminta and Fortune with the same relevance as the clothing they took with them. Thankfully, they were able to escape the servitude of this ruthless monster. However, if you want to learn more about their escape and how Rose Fortune came to be, you will have to read the book.

Special thanks to Brenda for telling Rose Fortune's story and sharing it with the world!

Maggie B. O'Donnell

Preface

I moved to the Annapolis Royal area in Nova Scotia on July 1, 1996. I had intended on living here only for the summer, and afterwards, my 11-year-old daughter Megan and I would move on to Vancouver, British Columbia, where several of my friends were working and living. I never left.

Within a week I had been told of two amazing women of this town; former mayor Daurene Lewis and her ancestor Rose Fortune. Within a month I met Daurene Lewis, who was such a strong and confident woman that I was initially intimidated by her. Her warmth, laughter and sense of humour soon overcame my trepidation and we got to know a bit about each other before she moved away to Halifax. I had heard and read about Daurene Lewis, the first female African-Canadian mayor in Canada, before I met her, but I was pleased to find out how proud the town of Annapolis Royal was of her and her accomplishments — as they also were of Rose Fortune.

I sought out more information on Rose Fortune, hoping to find a book, a documentary film, anything that would tell me more about her. I am a local history buff and particularly interested in the social history of Nova Scotian women. I found very little except rumours. Eventually, some documentary videos began appearing about Rose in the early 2000s but I could not find the written evidence to back up what was on the videos. Then a play was written about Rose, but the playwright admitted to using creative licence to make the story more dramatic.

As I was finishing up my book *A Wholesome Horror: Poor Houses in Nova Scotia* (SSP Publications, 2018), I spent a day in Halifax and had lunch with author Lance Woolaver. We were discussing what I should write next. Lance suggested that I write about Rose Fortune.

I jumped at the idea of researching and writing about Rose Fortune. When contacted by one of Rose's descendants, Maggie O'Donnell, my research took on a deeper intent, to include DNA testing.

I decided to write this book because of my fascination with the historical sociology of those who were not considered important under the status quo — that is, those who were not white, male, wealthy or even middle class, and thus, whose stories are not recorded in our history books. The story of Rose Fortune has been close to my heart since I moved to Annapolis Royal, the town and area I have come to settle in and love. I wanted to record her tale as accurately as possible, unearthing her life stories and giving her the respect she deserves. Rose Fortune was a woman of great stamina and dignity, who left an amazing legacy.

When writing about Rose Fortune, an African-Nova Scotian woman in the 18th and 19th centuries, I had to imagine what her life would have been like. As a 21st century woman who is not African-Nova Scotian, this presented a challenge. History has not been kind to African-Nova Scotian women in that there is little-to-no first voice recorded history. To put a voice to Rose, I read the narratives of people such as Boston King, who wrote a diary about living in Birch Town, Shelburne County in the 1780s, and Sojourner Truth, former slave and Abolitionist, along with "Memoir of Old Elizabeth, A Colored Woman and Other Testimonies of Women Slaves." Using their experiences and historical events happening at the time, I tried to tell the story of Rose and her family in 18th and 19th century Nova Scotia.

Throughout the book *Finding Fortune*, the use of the word "Negro" is used in context with the historical era. The phrase "Fugitive Black" is also used in accordance with the culture of the time. As the culture changes, so do the descriptors used for African-Nova Scotians. Occasionally a quote is used which describes African-Nova Scotians as "coloured" which was used during that era. Respect for African-Nova Scotians, while maintaining historical accuracy, was always the goal during the writing and editing of *Finding Fortune*.

Rose, thank you for the privilege of researching your life story and writing about you. My wish is for others to find out even more about you. I hope I've done you justice.

Acknowledgements

As any writer of history knows, I did not write this book alone. I had much help and guidance along the way. I thank my family, first and foremost, for the support and enthusiasm they give me when I take on a new book. Thank to you my parents, Richard and Juanita (Jess) Thompson, for reading over everything, pointing out any timeline errors and asking pertinent questions; to my daughters, Megan and Gwynneth Thompson, for being my cheering squad and to my husband, Kent Folks, for gently pushing aside my piles of papers and books on a corner of the kitchen table so that he could have his breakfast there before going to work, driving me to numerous book signings and being a great overall support.

My heartfelt thanks to Denise Rice and Wilfred Allan, who generously shared their research and worked to find more information when I needed it; thanks for the coffees and 'history nerd' talks. I hope we can continue. Huge thanks to Maggie B. O'Donnell for enthusiastically agreeing to take a DNA test and to her sister Ina Cromwell for agreeing to meet with me and sharing their family stories. Thanks to Debi Hill for agreeing to read over the manuscript from an African-Nova Scotian perspective. Thanks to James and Linda (Currie) Stevenson, my neighbours in Lequille, descendants both of Rose Fortune and who agreed to take a DNA test. To Lance Woolaver for suggesting this book and believing I could do this. Thanks to Barry Cahill, author and researcher of African-Nova Scotia history, for reading over my manuscript and letting me talk *ad nauseum* about the book over lunch. Thanks to the staff of the Nova Scotia Archives, who went out of their way to dig up old boxes filled with documents that hadn't been digitized. Thanks to Ian Lawrence, local historian and author, who challenged my research into Rose Fortune, causing me to dig deeper. Thanks to Wayne Smith, executive director of O'Dell House Museum in Annapolis Royal, for giving me support in conducting my research in the archives there. Thanks to Alan and Durline Melanson and The Historical Association of Annapolis Royal for promoting Rose Fortune and for making her a central figure in Annapolis and to the village of Inglewood for nominating Rose Fortune as the name of the new Digby Ferry. Thanks to Vanessa Fells, Dr. George Frempong and Russell

Grosse for being supportive and enthusiastic about this book. Thanks to my publisher, Scott Smith and SSP Publications, for giving me the green light and a contract to write about Rose Fortune.

Thanks to my editor, Brenda Conroy, who edits my mistakes and asks valuable questions to keep my work on track. Thank you to designer Gwen North, who works with historic images and documents that are not the easiest to work with. Last but not least, thank you to the Awesome Annapolis Foundation that gave me a small grant to do this book. This grant enabled me to purchase the DNA test kits, paid for my gas to travel to the Public Archives in Halifax and told me that the community believed in my book. Thank you for your faith in me.

Rose Fortune's Family Tree to the 4th Generation

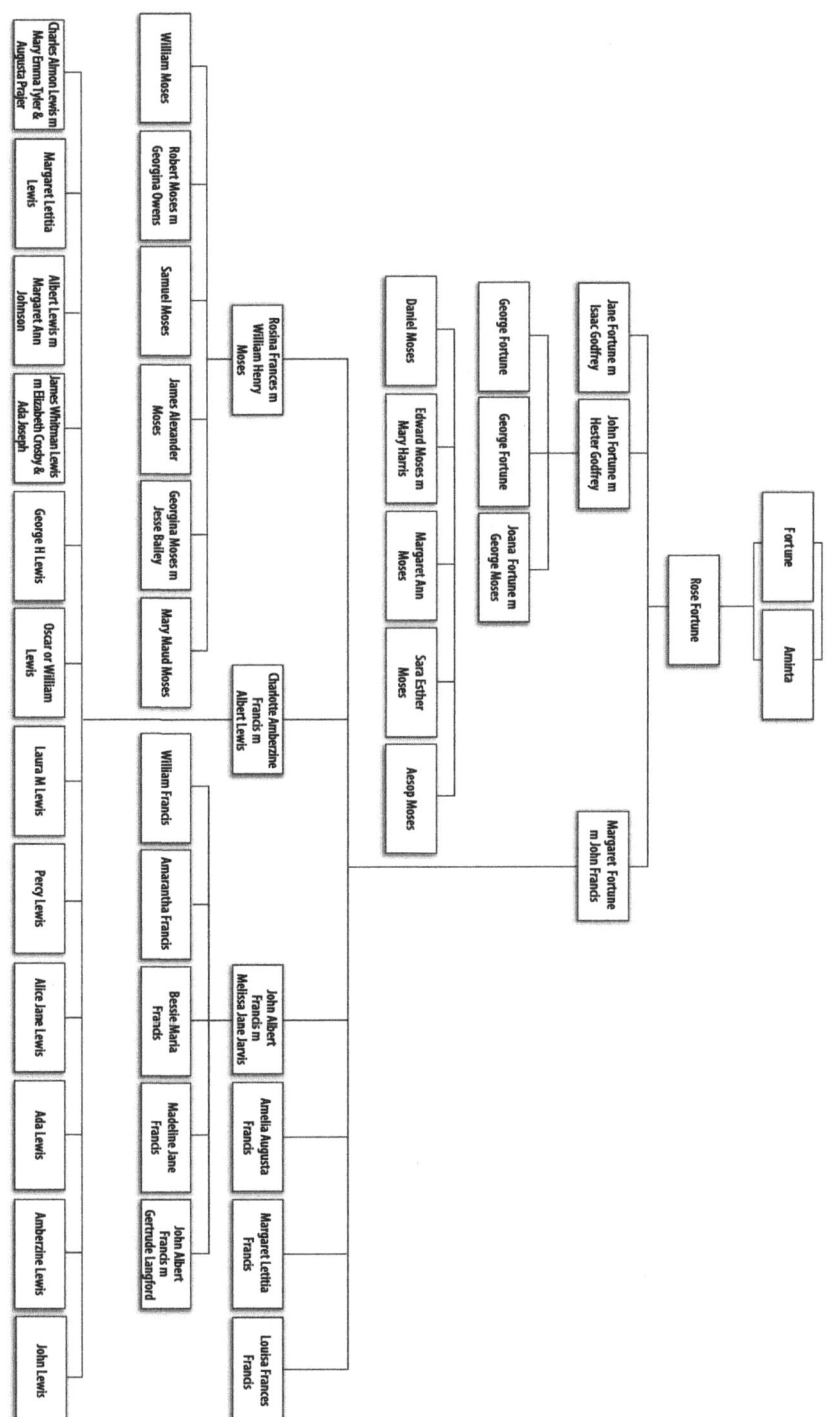

Prologue

They spooned under the hay while the wagon jostled them, creaking every time it hit a rock or hole. They kept as quiet as they could, scarcely breathing lest someone hear them. It was crucial that no one discover them in this wagon for they were fugitive slaves in Virginia, headed to the City of Brotherly Love, Philadelphia, on a fine morning in late April 1773.

They could hear the wagon stopping and the wagon driver Lucas greeting someone. He was talking with some men — white men. Their voices and accents gave them away. Lucas himself was white so he would not encounter any trouble from the men who stopped him.

"Lucas!" one of the men shouted. "We're looking for two runaways from Petersburg. A fella and a wench. You seen anything like that?"

"Nah," replied Lucas. "I ain't seen nothin' but birds and trees this morning. Been as quiet as can be."

"Well they ran off last night, according to Bradley," said another voice. "So, keep your eye out for them. There's a reward of 30 shillings if we can find them within 50 miles of his plantation."

"Ran off last night?" Lucas repeated. "Why, they could be anywhere by now! Down the Delaware River, or almost to Fredericksburg! Do you think those damned abolitionists are helping them?"

"We don't know yet," said someone else. "They coulda just run off on their own. But if we find out someone has been helpin' these darkies escape, we're gonna tar 'n feather 'em after we're done with them runaways."

"Well good luck lads. I can't help ya 'cause I've got to get this here hay off to Newton's and back again before my wife gets mad at me for dawdlin."

The men said goodbye and as Lucas gee-upped the horses, the man hiding in the hay felt one of the guys slap the side of the wagon. It had the ominous sound and impact that spoke of large hands with a great deal of strength.

Lucas started softly singing; the couple under the hay could hear him. He was singing Psalm 24; "The Earth is the Lord's, and everything in it…," their agreed-upon lyrics to let the fugitives know that the danger had passed. The woman finally let her breath out as they felt the wagon moving again. There would be many more of those tense moments to come in the following days.

The wagon crept on through fields and paths in the forests and finally, late in the evening when it was dark, Lucas brought the wagon into a barn. The man and woman were finally uncovered and allowed to stand, move around and have something to eat, for this was a safe house on the way north, to freedom. The couple still had a hard time believing that there were white people willing to support them in their escape. Their experiences with white people had not been good, especially when they had lived in Rhode Island with Captain Atkinson. They had both been abused by white people and had seen many other Negroes being so abused. Now some white people were trying to help them get to freedom. It didn't make a lot of sense to either of them, but here they were being helped, despite the laws against it. 'How do we know which white people to trust?', they asked themselves. They were helped first by Lucas, who they had approached. He was willing to help them escape the abuse of William Bradley, their master. Now they were helped by more white people, who were hiding them before moving them on to the next safe place, which might be a house, a church, a warehouse or a barn.

The man, Fortune, could not relax. He would not relax, he told himself, until he and his wife Aminta were in the north, at one of the communities where Negroes were allowed to be free. This line of sympathetic white folks was going to help him and Aminta get there, so they were told, if they would help themselves by running away. Fortune was still worried that this was all a set-up to get some reward money for turning them in after they run off, but his concerns were decreasing by the hour. Lucas and the other white folks seemed to genuinely want to help them.

After having something to eat and drink, the fugitives were hidden in a hole under the floor of the barn. The entrance was well hidden under horse droppings and hay in one of the stalls. Fortune and Aminta would stay there for a few hours and rest. Then they would be hidden in a box under the driver's seat of another wagon and taken to the next place of sanctuary. This would not be an easy fit for Fortune as he was nearly six feet tall. Aminta would be better off, as she was not even five feet in height. But they would endure it and everything else until they made it across the state line of Virginia into Pennsylvania, where they would head to Philadelphia.

In Petersburg, Virginia, William Bradley had been having a bad couple of months. Back in April, two of his most valuable slaves had run off together. Fortune and Aminta were hard workers and then they became lovers. Recently they had jumped the broom and become husband and wife. Bradley expected that they would have children and thereby increase the number of slaves that he that he would own or sell. But instead they ran off. Bradley had paid for advertisements for the return of Fortune and Amina to be published in the *Virginia Gazette* in April, but to date there had been no sign of either of them.

Bradley grumbled to himself that they were taking advantage of the fact that he had to be away from the plantation so often because of the political events raging in the Thirteen Colonies. The colonies just wanted to have freedom from taxation by those greedy British, who would just take their taxes and not spend it here in the colonies. "They probably put our taxes in the pockets of all those dandies, those earls and lords," Bradley grumbled to himself. "Those dandies just sit around all day in their finery, expecting other people to labour for them and then pay all their hard-earned monies to them in the form of taxes, while those dandies do nothing. I'm not doing all this work while someone else gets all the money," he thought, neglecting to see the irony, as he also grumbled about the money he paid for the runaway slave advertisement for Fortune and Aminta.

What was worse, he muttered, was that when he left the plantation in his wife's hands while he was gone to Williamsburg to do important political stuff, she wasn't as hard on the slaves as she should have been. "Her slackness is part of the reason that Fortune and Aminta ran off when they saw the chance," he ruminated. "She never did like the way I treated the slaves. Why, I should sell her just for being an irresponsible wife."

Two weeks later, William Bradley did just that! He took his wife to Winkworth Market and for two guineas and a silver watch, he sold her to George Ward. Bradley's wife did not complain, object, beg or even try to bargain with him. She didn't get on her knees with promises that she would be a better wife if only he wouldn't sell her. No, she did not. Bradley even put her in a halter to humiliate her in front of everyone at the market, walking her through from one end to the other, where Ward was waiting for them. Instead, his wife stood tall with dignity, walked with grace and did not even say goodbye to him when he left her there with Ward. Bradley walked away a bit surprised at what his wife did not do — she let Bradley leave her there and did not object. They had been married for 18 years. People were shocked that Bradley would do such a thing. "No wonder his slaves keep running away from him. If he treats his wife like that, how mean was he to his slaves," They knew full well what the answer was. The incident was so odd that it made the *Virginia Gazette* of June 17, 1773.

We hear from Derby, that laſt Week one William Bradley, of Mat-lock, ſold his Wife at Wirkſworth Market, for two Guineas and a Silver Watch, to George Ward, of the ſame Place, and delivered her in a Halter at the Market Croſs, paying a Sixpence for Toll. The above Couple had been married 18 Years.

Virginia Gazette, June 17, 1773 p. 2.

CHAPTER 1

Annapolis Royal, 1781 — just a couple of years before Rose and her parents landed there in 1783-84. Painted by Joseph Frederick Wallet DesBarres; Easson and Hoyt Collection, Public Archives of Nova Scotia.

Rose Arrives in Annapolis Royal

Rose could barely see over the wooden railing of the ship, but if she jumped up and down, she could catch a glimpse of the new town where she and her parents were going to live. She had her mother's height, or lack of it, and often had to climb on things or jump up to get the view she wanted. Right now, Rose was very excited to see where she and her parents would be living, owning land and being free. As the ship moved closer to the shore, Rose could discern more and more details. She could see a few low buildings close to the water at the bottom of a hill and a fort flying the British flag on top of the hill. Rose could see a lot of people along the water's edge; some were working, some were sitting with family members around them, others were watching the ships come up to the King's Wharf. There were many, many people in this small town. All along the shores of the basin she could see rough shanties and stretches of farmland. Beyond the town were rolling hills covered in green trees. Rose was not impressed.

Rose looked back at her mother and father as if to ask, "Can this be it?" Her mother, Aminta, was tending to her father, who could barely stand. He was leaning on his wife for support as he gazed at the new land that would welcome him and his family.

Fortune had been sick for a long time now and he did not seem to be getting any better. Rose and her mother hoped that the move would help him. Aminta was using all of the herbal remedies her own mother had taught her. The traditional healing methods, however, were not working on Fortune. He remained weak and sickly.

Fortune gazed intently at the scene before him. After coming from Philadelphia, the City of Brotherly Love, this view of Annapolis Royal was daunting. Wilderness stretched as far as the eye could see beyond the small gathering of huts on the shore of the town they called Annapolis Royal. It would mean freedom, however, for him and his family.

Or so he thought.

Fortune was depending on the promises of the British government, on Lord Dunmore's proclamation, which promised freedom to any enslaved African, or a rebel who escaped from his colonial master. Those who made it to the British lines would be forever free. After the war, even though the British lost, the "Negros" were declared free and offered refuge in a British colony. Fortune chose Nova Scotia as it was north of the Thirteen Colonies, which meant it would be colder but, Fortune reasoned, there was less chance of him and his family being caught and re-enslaved than if they went to Spanish Florida, Bermuda or the West Indies. "Rose was born free and will never know slavery so long as I breathe," he had promised himself when she was born, in Philadelphia in 1774.

"We've made it to the new land," Aminta whispered in Fortune's ear. "The new country where we'll be completely free. We'll have our own land, grow our own food, make our own money that we can keep for ourselves. You'll get better here with all this fresh air, not like in the dirty air of Philadelphia. Here we can find jobs and earn money; not like in Philadelphia."

Rose was not too certain about the promises that her mother was whispering in her father's ear. "Philadelphia may be dirty, but it is bigger than this place," she thought to herself. "Where are we going to live? There doesn't seem to be enough buildings for all the people on the shores and in the ships that are here and the ones that are coming."

Rose was absolutely right.

Documented Evidence of Rose Fortune's Arrival

Rose's concerns were justified. Annapolis Royal at the time of the arrival of the Loyalists was unprepared for the onslaught of thousands of people. It was a town of 120 people living in approximately thirty houses.[1] The town's inhabitants were mainly British, with a few Acadians who had returned after the Grand Dérangement of 1755-1764. During 1783, 2500 white Loyalists and a number of African-descended people arrived in Annapolis Royal from the northeast seaboard of the United States after Britain recognized the independence of the Thirteen Colonies in the Treaty of Paris.[2]

The Reverend Jacob Bailey, minister of the Church of England, had arrived in Annapolis Royal just a few years before the Loyalists came. A prodigious journal writer, Reverend Bailey recorded his life in Annapolis Royal and provided readers with a vivid description of the sudden arrival of thousands

Reverend Jacob Bailey, from *The Man Who Said No: Reading Jacob Bailey, Loyalist*, Kent Thompson (Gaspereau Press, 2008).

of Loyalists, some with their Black slaves. Freed Blacks and American fugitive slaves arrived as well. On Saturday, October 19, 1782 the first five hundred Loyalists and passengers arrived at the King's Wharf in eleven ships.[3] Many more ships were to come, including the one that carried Fortune, Aminta and Rose.

Although the British offered freedom to any 'Negro' who escaped their rebel masters, this did not mean that the British were abolitionists. The British allowed Loyalists to bring their

Black slaves with them to Nova Scotia. Among those enslaved Africans were people owned by the family of James DeLancey. Historian Harvey Amani Whitfield writes: 'James DeLancey, from one of the most wealthy and famous families in New York, brought about six slaves to Annapolis. He continued the practice of slave holding throughout his life'.[4] James DeLancey went on to become a Member of the Legislative Assembly (MLA) and Speaker of the House.[5] Another of the many Loyalists who brought enslaved African people was the Davoue family. Frederick Davoue senior brought at least two slaves with him to Annapolis.[6] He left his son, Frederick Davoue Jr., behind in New York, and he carried on the tradition of slave-holding in that state.[7]

Rose's Family Meets Joseph Leonard

Rose and her parents surveyed the scene before them as they stood on the glebe land in this new town of Annapolis Royal. All of their belongings were at their feet. Around them was a bustle of people, some Black, some white, some native Mi'kmaq. Many had erected tents and started cooking fires. Children were running and playing everywhere. Fortune looked at the chaos and confusion, wondering where to go, who to speak with to arrange shelter for his family. Finally, he stopped a man with warm brown eyes.

"Excuse me," he said. "Name is Fortune. I'm a free man. This is my family. And I am wondering who I am supposed to speak with to arrange shelter for ourselves."

The man, not as tall as Fortune but with a kindly face, chuckled at the question. "Welcome, Fortune," he said. "Name is Joseph Leonard. I am a churchman. Can I help you brother?"

Fortune knew he had chosen wisely in stopping this man, for he and his family were followers of the Church of England as well. They had been since they had escaped to the township of Devone, outside the city of Philadelphia.

"Yes," said Fortune. "I've been mighty sick and my wife and child here, we need shelter and food. Can we find some place to stay till I heals up and feels better?"

"Shelter is rare here, Fortune," Leonard said sadly. "This town was un-prepared for all of the Loyalists and us free Negroes landing on their shores. Seems no one told 'em we were coming. There is only shelter for the rich Loyalists and none for us and our families. The houses, the church, the tavern

— even the barracks is all filled up with white people, the Loyalists from down south. Food is scarce, wood is scarce, help is scarce. We Negro settlers need to stick together and fend for ourselves."

Fortune felt the first pangs of disappointment settle in his chest. And panic. What could they do? He was still so sick and weak and he needed to protect his wife and daughter. Aminta stepped forward.

"Mr. Leonard, we would be much obliged if you would be able to help us in any kind of way that you can because, as you can see, my husband is very ill."

"Of course," Leonard responded. "I forgot my manners. I am sorry. I was just looking at your face. You do not look like most of the Negroes I have seen around here."

Aminta smiled at his observation. "That is because my grandmother was from the shores of Great Spain. I am part Andean," she responded.

"That must be where your long straight hair comes from," he mused. "Well, come along with me and let us find some shelter for your man and child."

Leonard led them to a large tent where a number of Negroes were working and milling about. Sitting down by one of the open fires, Leonard had one of the women ladle out a tin cup of broth for each of them. Leonard asked them where they had come from. As Fortune and Aminta filled him in, Rose looked around at the other children. Looking back to the adults in conversation, she caught her mother's eye, who nodded that she could go and play with them. Rose smiled for the first time since seeing Annapolis Royal.

Rose and her family spent their first night in Annapolis bundled under their clothes for warmth as they slept on the ground in Leonard's shared tent. They were luckier than most. Many of the Negro people had only the clothes on their backs to keep them warm. Rose lay on the ground, huddled up to her mother and father for warmth and security. She wondered what would become of their new life in this land and when her father would get better.

The next day, after Leonard had spoken with some of the leaders of the camp, he came to check on Fortune, Aminta and Rose. Aminta and Rose had erected their own shelter and built their own fire pit and Leonard brought them some warm broth for breakfast.

Leonard explained that anyone who killed some food, such as a rabbit, moose, squirrels, anything, must bring it to the communal tent to be shared amongst all the Negroes — same with wood for fires. With the cold weather promising to come soon, they would start building huts for families and everyone was expected to pitch in and help.

"When will we get the land we were promised," asked Fortune, "and where will it be?"

"Only the Black Pioneers were promised land," answered Leonard. "And we Negro folk can count on not getting our provisions until the white folk are taken care of."

Fortune and Aminta thought upon this: "Well, we may be poor," Fortune mused out loud, "but at least we are free."

Leonard snorted out loud. "We are free alright. Let's just make sure it stays that way."

Rose was startled by this statement. She looked to her parents. Fortune looked sharply at Leonard. Aminta held her breath. "What do you mean?" Fortune asked. "We are free Negroes here, aren't we?"

"Some of us are, some of us aren't," Leonard answered. "Lots of these Loyalists brought their slaves. Why, one of the heroes of the Loyalists, a man named Ruggles, he brought nine slaves with him. He's intending to set up a plantation on the North Mountain here, just like the one he left behind in the colonies down south. And just a few months ago, a couple of slaves, husband and wife, ran away from their master. They hid in a barn just over there," he said, pointing to a scorched piece of land down the hill from the glebe land they were sitting on, close to a bog, "and somehow it caught fire. Most likely an accident. They got charged and convicted of burning it down on purpose. They were hanged over there on Hog Island for that," he said, pointing to a small island in the river. "And just a few weeks ago, before you arrived here, a Negro fella named Boice was also hanged. I can't remember what for — probably for being Black."

"Nah, Fortune," Leonard said, "this is no promised land for Negro folk. The British just wanted our sweat, our work, to help them fight the revolutionaries. Didn't matter if they won or lost, they were never gonna give much of a damn about us once the matter was dealt with." Leonard chuckled derisively. "Matter of fact, you might want to consider changing your name, Fortune. I've known a coupla slaves named Fortune and not a one of them felt like they was lucky or fortunate."

Rose watched her parents as they stared down at their feet in dismay. These were the feet that brought them to what they thought would be freedom and equality. Surely it couldn't be that bad, they told themselves.

It was.

Evidence of Rose's Family in the Area

Fortune, Aminta and Rose may have arrived in Annapolis Royal in 1783, but Fortune does not show up on any documents regarding the settlement of Loyalists and Freed Negroes until 1784. The Muster Roll of discharged officers, disbanded soldiers and Loyalists taken in Annapolis County from June 18 to 24, 1784, shows 'Fortune — a free Negro' and makes note of a woman with him and a child under the age of ten.[8] This entry is most certainly in reference to Rose and her parents. Annapolis County, in those days, was one of the five original counties of Nova Scotia and included the area we now know as the Town and County of Digby. The County of Digby was not separated from Annapolis County until 1837.[9]

Fortune was the slave name of Rose's father. Aminta was her mother's slave name. Neither had a surname. Although many formerly enslaved people took on a surname, with some, such as the Ruggles, taking on the surname of their former masters, many did not claim either their former master's name or any surname. In the case of fugitive slaves, their former master's surname might make it easier to find them. Many of the Black families that were recorded as arriving in Nova Scotia were listed as 'servants', not 'slaves'. Methodist minister and historian T.W. Smith argues in his writings that 'servants' and 'slaves' were basically the same thing:

> Still-enslaved Negroes brought by the Loyalist owners to the Maritime Provinces in 1783 and 1784 were classed as "servants" in some of the documents of the day. Lists of Loyalist companies bound for Shelburne, made out, it is probable, under the direction of British officers whose dislike of the word "slave" would lead them to use the alternative legal terms, contain columns for "men, women, children and servants" the figures in the "servants" column being altogether disproportionate to those in the preceding columns.[10]

Often these 'servants' did not have surnames, which could be an indicator of enslavement. How do we tell the difference between 'servants' and 'slaves'? Whitfield suggests:

Scholars must recognize the ambiguity and subtleties of the terminology used in the primary source material … Boisseau was from South Carolina and brought five Black "servants" with no surnames from the Lowcountry. These servants were likely slaves … On the same muster, under the category of servants, a few such as Thom Webster seem to have been white, but many in the servant category were listed as blacks with no surnames including Bristol, William, Nanny, Stafford, Collins, Harry, Cesar, and Alexander.[11]

Many historians and researchers, myself included, have mistakenly researched while wearing white Anglo-Saxon Protestant lenses, with an assumption of a surname when looking for Rose's family. It is only after removing the lenses that we realize that not all people, and certainly not all African-descended people, had a surname.

Rose was born into freedom and was not, to our knowledge or research, ever enslaved. Among the rumours regarding Rose and her family was the idea that they had escaped from a family named Devone, who lived outside of the city of Philadelphia.[12] Although Philadelphia and the state of Pennsylvania still had legalized slavery in the 1770s, when Rose's family escaped to this area, it was the second state to enact gradual abolition in 1780, with Massachusetts leading the way.[13]

Philadelphia by 1774 had a small but vocal population of religious people known as Quakers, also known as the Society of Friends. Although the Quakers had originally brought enslaved Africans with them to the New World from England in the 1660s, gradually many of them began to see slavery as a violation of their religious beliefs.[14] Many Quakers began 'manumitting' —freeing their slaves voluntarily. Other enslaved people negotiated with their owners for freedom and still others ran away from their owners, thus playing a large part in bringing about the abolition of slavery.[15] Whitfield writes: "The focus on slavery's peripheral existence and eventual death is understandable, but it underestimates the role Black people played in freeing themselves from bondage … Black people had a great deal of agency in freeing themselves. Judges chipped away at the system, but people of African descent initiated the process by running away from their owners at great personal risk."[16] Fortune and Aminta ran away from their owner, thus freeing themselves from bondage without waiting for legislation or permission.[17]

With the combination of gradual abolition laws, private manumissions and fugitives from slavery from Pennsylvania and other states, the growth of a free Black population was centred in the state and particularly in and around Philadelphia. One of the townships that existed in 1774 just outside the city was named Devon.

History, particularly oral history, can get lost, remade and reconstructed and is sometimes downright wrong. Often, however, there is a grain of truth behind the tales. The problem lies in finding that grain. My research has not unearthed any slave-owning family named Devone, Divine, Deveau, Deveaux or DeVoe in either the state of Pennsylvania or the state of Virginia. The slave-owning families with any of those names were mainly located along the Hudson River in the state of New York, with one family, Frederick Davoue, arriving in Annapolis Royal with his slaves from New York with the Loyalists.[18] A placard in the Daurene Lewis Plaza at the Town Hall of Annapolis Royal suggests that Rose Fortune came to Annapolis Royal with the Davoue family in 1783.

> This singular woman (possibly born in Virginia on 13 March 1774) likely came to Nova Scotia with the slave-holding Davoue family (Devoe, Devost, Devone) following the American Revolution.[19]

If you ponder this statement, questions arise. The Davoue family is noted as arriving with two slaves — one male and one female,[20] to a land that needed a great deal of physical labour to start farming. Having as many enslaved labourers as possible would only make economic and practical sense to slave owners. Why would Frederick Davoue, who believed in slavery, manumit more than half of his slaves while keeping others? Whitfield notes in his paper *Slavery in English Nova Scotia 1750–1810* that '…..versatile and multi-occupational slaves were essential for Nova Scotia slaveholders'.[21] The fact that Fortune, who was noted as with a wife and child, was listed in

1784 on the Muster Roll as being 'a free Negro' also negates the history on the memorial placard.

Could it be that the oral history of Rose and her family running away from a slave-owning family named Devone was wrong and that Rose and her family were actually free and living in the township of Devon, Pennsylvania? Historian C. Herbert Fry wrote that the residents of Devon and Easttown were Church of England, not Quakers. "Their church, Old St. David's, constructed in 1715, lies just outside the borders of Easttown in Newton Township."[22] Rose and her family were followers of the Church of England, as were most of the Loyalists who arrived in Nova Scotia. The story of Devon had likely become twisted in the multiple re-telling of Rose's story. There were many more rumours to examine about Rose's life as it unfolded in Annapolis County.

In my fictional account of Fortune and his family meeting up with Joseph Leonard, the story of the escaped slaves who were hanged is true. William Calnek and Alfred Savary record the story in an appendix in their 1897 book *The History of the County of Annapolis:*

> In 1783 a coloured man named Ellis and his wife were, sad to relate, executed at Annapolis. They had taken refuge in a barn near the site of the skating rink, and setting it on fire, caused its destruction with its contents, and were found guilty by a jury of the crime of arson, and hanged on Hog Island. In 1784 a coloured man named Boice was executed, I do not know for what offence.[23]

The conditions in Annapolis Royal when Rose and her family arrived were extremely difficult. The existing buildings were filled to capacity with Loyalists, their families and their belongings. The Black community was indeed left to find shelter and food and to fend for themselves. Annapolis Royal was overwhelmed. Reverend Jacob Bailey's observations reflect this in his journal of 1784:

> The Regiment quartered in Annapolis are perpetually engaged in stealing and plundering the property of their neighbours ... Besides these martial sons we have disbanded soldiers, sailors, free Negroes, sturdy villains from the continent, and even some of the pious inhabitants of

Nova Scotia ...... the free Negroes are excusable more than any other denomination of thieves since they are allowed no provisions, a circumstance which has reduced them to a starving condition — unless some speedy relief is afforded them, they might perish by scores with hunger.[24]

Slavery was still legal in Nova Scotia and Loyalist Timothy Ruggles, considered one of the Loyalist heroes of the American Revolution, is recorded as bringing several slaves with him to Nova Scotia in 1783.[25] In 2012, Dr. Catherine M.A. Cottreau-Robins wrote her thesis for her interdisciplinary PhD specifically on the Ruggles plantation, located in what is now known as Spa Springs in Wilmot, Annapolis County.[26] According to Whitfield, 'slavery existed in most parts of the colony, but was particularly strong in Shelburne and the Annapolis region'.[27] Thus, Rose and her parents and any other 'free Negroes' were vulnerable to re-enslavement despite promises made to them by the British. Whitfield writes:

The line between slavery and freedom in late eighteenth and early nineteenth century Nova Scotia was fluid and contingent ... The Black Loyalists were only nominally free and could easily slip back into a state of slavery. They were Black, like their enslaved brethren, and this racial identity was more significant in deciding their place in society as opposed to whether they were free nor not.[28]

In her unpublished but excellent paper *Stark Remnants of Blackpast: Thinking on Gender, Ethnicity and Class in 1780s Nova Scotia*, J.A. Mannette wrote: 'The free Blacks who came to Nova Scotia may have indeed been legally free. However, in the minds of most white Nova Scotians of all classes they were associated with, and treated like, their enslaved brethren ... Thus, free Blacks came to share the status of slaves'.[29]

The colonial government of Nova Scotia was not equipped to deal with the sudden influx of thousands of Loyalists, their slaves and freed Negroes who arrived here following the end of the Revolutionary War in the United States. The Loyalists were promised land grants but the system was inefficient, class-based, gender-based and colour-biased.[30] Mannette writes: 'In a system which had as its aim the first and largest recompense to those who had lost the most, in terms of property, the formerly property-less Blacks were low on the list of priorities'.[31]

In addition to being assumed to be a slave because of their colour, free Blacks had to worry about being claimed as a slave by a white person who wanted their labour. If Black settlers were busy doing their own farming, building, fishing or business, they might not be available to work for whites.[32] Quoting historian John Grant, Mannette writes: 'If a Black man were claimed as a slave by a white man, his wife and children were claimed as well'.[33]

The white fear of freed Black people becoming self-sufficient on the land given to them by the colonial government was largely a moot point. The Black populations were not only the last to receive their land grants, if they received them at all they also received the worst land on which to farm. Birchtown, (Shelburne County) Brinley Town (now called Jordanville, outside the town of Digby) and Little Tracadie in Guysborough County 'were the only all-Black settlements in Loyalist Nova Scotia and the only grants of land made directly to free black people'.[34] The best land for agriculture, mainly in the Annapolis Valley, was quickly grabbed up by the richest Loyalists, who were promised, on average, a grant of 100 acres for the family head and an additional 50 acres for each family member — wife, son, daughter and slave.[35] The Black settlers received less acreage than the whites, with clear title rarely being given to them. In Brinley Town, the Freed Blacks received, on average, two acres per family, on soil that was acidic and thin.[36] It was rare for Black women to be given land acreage in their own name. Mannette writes:

> Their farm lots were often located so far from the town lots they were given that is was difficult to get to them, let alone develop them … Blacks were seen primarily as a source of labour for whites, their need for land was questionable … [Thus] we can understand the lack of clear title to land for Blacks, the relatively smaller size of the lots they received and the location of Black settlements situated conveniently close to white towns such as Shelburne.[37]

This was for the purpose of Black workers being able to walk to the white town and work for whites in their houses and farms, but then walking back to their community outside of town. Thus, white people could use the Blacks for their work but did not have to have Blacks as their neighbours. In the case of Annapolis County, the Black community of Brinley Town and what would eventually become Lequille were conveniently located outside the towns of Digby and Annapolis Royal respectively. There was a Black settlement outside the village of Granville Ferry, settled by sons and daughters of freed Blacks.[38] Little Tracadie (Guysborough County) is noted as being the only major freed Black settlement that was not "envisioned as a satellite community for the convenience of a larger white town because of its isolation."[39]

Rose, however, bucked the trend and lived in the town of Annapolis Royal, on and off, for many years. But tragedy would stalk her family before they even settled in the area of Annapolis County.

CHAPTER 2

Fortune and Aminta Meet; Rhode Island to Virginia

Fortune stood on the deck of the ship with other Negro men, chained to each other, and watched as the women slaves were brought on board. They were also bound together and were forced to move as one because of the shortness of the chains that held them. Although they were clothed in dresses and shawls, some with their hair wrapped in traditional African wraps, it was not enough to protect them from the cold November winds of Rhode Island. One woman in particular caught Fortune's eye. She was small in stature but had very long black hair down her back, almost to her buttocks. Instead of being a deep ebony colour like most of the Africans on the ship, her skin was like caramel, but she had the facial characteristics of an African woman — high proud cheekbones and dark flashing eyes.

Captain John Atkinson shouted out orders and got their attention. He informed everyone that his crew would be moving them down below deck to the berths, and once they were in place, the ship would be moving out. He warned the enslaved men and women to behave themselves or he would not hesitate to force them overboard and let them find their own way ashore. They did not know where they were going and the tension was already high.

Fortune moved below deck with the others. As the ship's crew moved them down the stairs, their chains still attached, Fortune whispered to one of the crew, "Where are we going?" The sailor looked around quickly to make sure none of the other crew members saw him talking to one of the slaves. The other sailors were distracted with their duties. "Virginia," he whispered.

Fortune quietly passed the word on to other slaves and news soon got around that they were sailing to Virginia to be sold to plantation owners. Some of the people were newly brought from Africa and did not understand English or the geography of the Thirteen Colonies on the eastern continent of this side of the Atlantic Ocean. This foreign word "Virginia" meant nothing to them except more fear and confusion. But Fortune and many of the other enslaved Africans knew what the word meant: plantations. And plantations meant back-breaking work and an early death. Fortune had heard that many slaves did not last more than five years because the owners worked them so hard. He sighed with resignation and hoped this life would be over soon and that he would move on to a better life.

When Aminta heard that they were being moved to Virginia, she also knew what that meant. She would be either in the field or in the house of the owner, and Aminta didn't know which she'd prefer. The field was very hard work; however, the house meant she would have to be available all hours of the day and night. "It does not matter where I am, field or house," she told herself, "I could be raped by any of them." She tried to remain strong and subdue the sobs of worry and fear in her chest. She missed her mother and sisters and cried quietly to herself. She slept fitfully, with the heavy chains causing her great discomfort.

Fortune and Aminta stood chained together on the shores of the town of Williamsburg, Virginia. They had been sold to the same owner, William Bradley of Petersburg. He was a short, balding, mean-looking man; white with blue eyes the colour of a frozen winter sky. He physically examined Fortune and Aminta, squeezing her breasts and his testicles. He looked at their teeth and eyes like he was purchasing a horse. After he bought them, Bradley took the chain that bound them together and added another length of chain which he attached to the back of the horse-drawn cart. Not saying a word to either of them, he gee-upped the horses and moved the cart along. Fortune and Aminta were forced to walk behind the cart. Fortune tried to talk with Aminta but as soon as he asked her a question, Bradley barked, "No talking." Fortune and Aminta looked at each other and were silent for the rest of the dusty trip north from Williamsburg.

The walk only took a few hours and they were at the plantation, their new home. It wasn't as big as other plantations, with only a few dwellings in the slave quarters area. Aminta was shown to a hut with another family and Fortune was sent to bunk down with other single men.

The next few weeks were a blur of learning what the owner expected, working out in the fields, learning the other slaves' names and personalities. But mostly they were getting to know each other. Aminta worked in both the field and in the house helping Mrs. Bradley. Mrs. Bradley wasn't a southern woman who lay around barking orders at slaves; she worked alongside Aminta in the house, cleaning and preparing meals. Mind you, Aminta did the hardest of the labour, and although Mrs. Bradley had warmed to her, it did not stop her from yelling if she felt Aminta wasn't working hard or fast enough. Aminta did notice, however, that whenever Mr. Bradley left the plantation for meetings or business, Mrs. Bradley did not work so hard and tended to take advantage of Mr. Bradley's absence by having afternoon naps and letting the work slide a bit.

Fortune, meanwhile, worked with the animals as well as planting, hoeing and harvesting in the fields. As Fortune was tall and dignified-looking, Bradley often had him change into house clothes and tend to the door when guests arrived. Sometimes, when Bradley was going to a business or political meeting and wanted to show off, he made Fortune wear a uniform and drive the carriage to the meeting. For slaves, both Aminta and Fortune had more than the usual amount of clothing to fulfil all their work roles. When all hands were needed, everyone except Mr. and Mrs. Bradley were in the fields.

In the evenings, the labourers gathered around their community fire to talk quietly in their fatigue, sing inspirational songs to keep their spirits up or just reflect on their lives. It was here that Fortune and Aminta finally spoke with each other.

"Aminta, where did you get that hair from? And your colour? We all of us here," he swept his arm about to include everyone around the fire, "are as black as night but you, you're the colour of a coffee bean and your lips are smaller."

Aminta chuckled softly with delight that he was so interested. "My mother was from the Spanish Main when she was captured as a slave." she answered. "Her people were brown, not black. But my father was from Africa so I am a mixture of bloods."

She looked at Fortune. "And what about you, Fortune?" she asked. "Your nose is as straight and narrow as a walkway but you are as black as an African. Where did you get that nose from?"

"I have no idea," he answered simply. "I have heard rumours that my people not only came from Africa, but also from some land on the other side of Africa."

They smiled, warm eyes admiring each other.

Aminta looked to the fire. "My name is actually Aminata," she said. "My father named me before he was sold away from my mother and sisters. He was Swahili and said the word *Aminata* means 'serenity'. But my little sisters had a hard time pronouncing my name and kept calling me Aminta, so I became Aminta."

"I've never heard of such a name before," Fortune said. "It's beautiful."

"Which one?" Aminta asked teasingly.

"Both," he said. "Which name do you want to be called?"

Aminta thought for a moment. "I think I want to stay with Aminta," she answered. "It reminds me of my little sisters and makes me smile."

"Well then, Aminta," Fortune smiled at her. "My name is Fortune, as you already know. I wasn't named by my father or mother. My owner named me Fortune. I don't know if that is because I have always been big and strong and he expected me to make him a fortune or because he thought I would eat him out of victuals and cost him a fortune!"

They both chuckled.

The months went on and Fortune and Aminta fell into friendship and love. Mrs. Bradley noted the happiness and sparkling eyes of Aminta and soon figured out what was happening. She told Mr. Bradley, who had no sense of romance.

"Good," he said. "They are both a bit older but it's not too late for them to breed and give me more slaves."

Mrs. Bradley turned her head, rolling her eyes at her husband's mercenary ways.

Fortune and Aminta as Fugitives

Fortune and Aminta were in love and decided they wanted to live together. Bradley was more than happy to accommodate this relationship and had the other slaves build a hut for them. The slaves had a marriage celebration when Fortune and Aminta jumped the broom and moved into their hut together. "Now you'll have babies to love and keep you warm if the master don't sell them," one of the women said to Aminta, thinking she was giving her wishes for a good future.

Aminta immediately froze. She had always wanted to avoid having children for just that reason. But she had never told Fortune. What would he think — to not have any sons or daughters? And as they were both getting older, their time for children would be running out in just a few years.

That evening, after the celebration party left their hut, Aminta held her hand up to Fortune's chest.

"Before we do anything, Fortune," she said seriously, "I should have talked to you about this earlier, and I'm sorry."

Fortune was concerned. "What is wrong Aminta?"

"I am not having any babies to be sold away from us nor to grow up to be slaves," she said. "I couldn't bear it. I watched what my mother and other mothers have gone through and I can't do it. I have taken enough of a risk falling in love with you. Why do you think I am the age I am without a man? Because I didn't want to fall in love and then see my husband sold away from me. It's bad enough that that could happen even now, but I don't want to lose babies as well as you. My heart would just break."

Fortune smiled a great big grin.

"It's not funny, Fortune," Aminta protested.

"No, it's not funny," Fortune agreed, losing his smile. "I'm sorry. But you just brought up the very same idea that I had. We are not going to have babies only to have them sold away as slaves. We are not going to have babies until we are free."

Aminta looked at him as if he were crazy. "Free?" she replied. "Well you know that is never going to happen. We're in Virginia now and it's as bad as Rhode Island."

"Yes, we're in Virginia now," he answered. "But I found out that Virginia is only one state south from Pennsylvania. And in Pennsylvania is Philadelphia. And in Philadelphia, there is a group of people called Quakers. And these here Quakers have not only set all their slaves free but are banging on the government to set all slaves free. Why, they even have communities of free Negroes!"

Aminta was shocked. "Free Negroes? Whole communities of us? Free? And the white folks put up with that?"

"Well, some don't," Fortune admitted, "but the ones that do outnumber the ones that don't. And the state is making laws about abolition ... making all Negro folks free from slavery. And they are only one state north of us."

"That must be some kind of place," said Aminta, still stunned by the idea of Negroes living together, free, doing work only for themselves and not for white people.

"And that is where we are gonna run away to," Fortune smiled.

"Run away?" Aminta snapped out of her reverie about free Negro communities. "How are we going to run away? We don't even know which direction to go. Bradley will put a hunt out for us and if we are caught, he will sell one of us away. It'd break my heart and we only just wed."

Fortune smiled again. "But I know what way to take. And I know how we are going to escape. You know, I've been working with Cleo, and I got to trust him and his knowledge. I asked him if anyone on this here plantation has ever run away. He looked at me sharp-like and asked me direct: 'You plannin' on running, Fortune?' 'Maybe', I said, 'maybe not.'"

"Cleo said that he thought of runnin' plenty of times but now he's got Fanny, his wife, and his kids, and Fanny is havin' another one, so he is staying. 'But I know a white guy who helps slaves escape,' Cleo said. 'A white guy who helps slaves escape?' I was astonished," said Fortune.

Aminta snorted with disbelief and disgust. "Why would a white person help us? They just want our work and our children."

"But that's just it," Fortune replied. "Some white folks are believing that slavery is an evil that God is against. They believe that they won't go to Heaven unless they do something to stop slavery. These white folks are believing what these Quakers have been saying, and it's even spread down here. And Cleo said he can make arrangements to get this white guy, Lucas, to help us escape."

A couple of weeks later, Fortune slipped off into the forest and met with Lucas. It was a quick and quiet meeting.

"I know a buncha white folk all along the route north," Lucas said. "I can get you to folk that'll hide you, feed you and send you on to the next safe house."

"Why would they do this?" Fortune asked. "What's in it for them?"

"Slavery ain't right," said Lucas. "It's a sin. And I want to get to Heaven to see my son that died five years ago. So I'm working against sin as the Lord would want me to do. I'm working to free all you darkies that will take the chance of running. Mind you, I'm taking a chance too, but you'll be whipped if we're caught. Me and my wife would be shunned by our neighbours and maybe even charged by the law and have to move to another town, but at least we'll still be free. And if I do this, I'll get to see my son. Our preacher tells me it's in the Bible."

Fortune and Lucas made plans for two days later. Bradley was going into Williamsburg for another political meeting. He had already told Fortune that he needed him planting in the field instead of driving him. Fortune and Aminta were to hide some food and clothing in the woods at their meeting spot near the road. Then Lucas would come with a wagon load of hay, which they would crawl into, and he would take them on the first leg of their journey to freedom.

Two days later, Fortune and Aminta slipped away from the fields in the low afternoon light and ran into the dark forest. They hid behind fallen trees near the road, where they had put some clothes and food the night before. Soon they heard the sound of the wagon drawing near. Fortune and Aminta came out of hiding with their possessions.

"Lawd a Goshen!" Lucas exclaimed. "Y'all got a lotta clothes for slaves!"

"Well if they don't know what clothes we're wearing today or tomorrow, the white folks won't know what to look for," Fortune answered. "Plus we can sell them for food if we need to."

Aminta and Fortune crawled under the hay and made themselves as comfortable and as hidden as they could. They were too scared to eat. They knew that Bradley would put the word out that they ran away as soon as he noticed they were gone.

Lucas gee-upped the horses and the wagon moved on. He brought them to his own barn the first night, locking them in and telling them they could get up to relieve themselves and to eat, but that was all. They were to get right back under the hay as soon as they'd done that. They would start out again at morning's first light. They were not to make a sound, no matter what the circumstances.

Bradley came home from Williamsburg late that night. His wife was already asleep in her room. The slaves were all abed and sleeping as well. He crawled into his bed, exhausted from all the political fighting, arguing and shouting.

The next day, he got up late, for him. Drinking his coffee on the back verandah, he called for Cleo.

"Yas suh," said Cleo, head down, knowing what was coming.

"Send Fortune over to me," Bradley said. "I want him to drive me over to Johnson's house and I want to make a good impression."

"Fortune ain't here, suh," Cleo responded.

"Well, where is he?" Bradley demanded.

"Dunno, suh," Cleo answered, not offering any further information.

"Did you see him at breakfast victuals this morning?"

"No, suh."

Bradley was becoming alarmed. "Was Fortune at supper last night?"

"No, suh," Cleo responded.

"Goddamn!" Bradley jumped up and threw the remainder of his coffee on the ground and ran into the house to send out word of a runaway slave. It was then that he found out from his wife that her girl, Aminta, was not to be found anywhere either. Bradley roared with rage. As he didn't have any dogs, he would have to borrow some to sniff out their trail. He immediately sent Cleo off to one of the neighbours, with a note saying he had runaways and he needed to borrow their dogs and expertise. Cleo took his time going to the neighbours, stopping to admire some leaves, pick a few mushrooms and then he ran into the neighbour's yard, acting as if he was out of breath.

While he waited for the neighbour to arrive with the dogs, Bradley sat down and wrote a runaway slave advertisement for the *Virginia Gazette*. He had his wife go look in their hut and see what they took with them. They took everything. Bradley wrote a long ad and sent a slave on his fastest horse to Williamsburg to have it posted in the next edition of the newspaper. The horse was not fast enough; Bradley missed the week's edition of the *Gazette* and had to wait until the next week.

The neighbour arrived with the dogs and some more neighbours to help find the runaways. At times like this, they reasoned, everyone must pitch in. If not, all their slaves would be running away. The dogs would track them down fast. And track them down fast they did — to a spot just beyond a fallen down tree, where the smell of the fugitive slaves was lost in the middle of the road.

"They're in a wagon," Bradley quickly concluded. "But whose? They's lotsa wagons around here."

A week later, the *Virginia Gazette* published Bradley's advertisement, calling on the good citizens and masters of vessels to return his runaway slaves.

To make sure that they would be found, Bradley included a great deal of information about what his runaways looked like, special features that made them distinguishable, the clothes that they wore and the clothes they took with them.

Runaway slave advertisement for Fortune and Aminta, believed to be the parents of Rose Fortune. *Virginia Gazette*, Williamsburg, Virginia. April 29, 1773

PETERSBURG, April 21, 1773, Run away, last Night, from the Subscriber, two Slaves, namely: A Negro Fellow named FORTUNE, about six Feet high, slim made, has a thin Nose for one so Black as he is, and appears to be about forty Years of Age; he took with him sundry Wearing Apparel, particularly a Pair of Buckskin Breeches almost new, a Thickset Coat, a brown Sailor's Jacket, a red great Coat, a fine Hat, pretty much worn, with a large Brim, and commonly has it cocked up, wears a red Worsted Cap in common, and sometimes a Silk one. Also a Wench named AMINTA, appears to be about thirty Years of Age, short and well made, has much the Look of an Indian, and is so, her Mother having been brought from the Spanish Main to Rhode Island, has long Black Hair, which she wears in her Neck, and took with her a Black Quilt, a red Flannel Petticoat, a dark Ground Calico Gown, a blue and white one, and an old light coloured Stuff ditto, a red Cardinal, a Black Bonnet, and several other Things. I lately had them of Captain John Atkinson, and as they were brought from Rhode Island, it is probable they will endeavour to get there again, as they pretend to Freedom. I request it as a Favour of all Masters of Vessels not to harbour or entertain them, as it will probably be attended with bad Consequences. I will give a Reward of Three Pounds if they are taken fifty Miles from home and secured so that I my get them again, and THIRTY SHILLINGS if within that Distance. WILLIAM BRADLEY

Documentation of Fugitive Slaves

Did Fortune and Aminta escape from Virginia by hiding in a wagon load of hay? Did they run away under the darkness of night? We might never know the answers to these questions, as they have not, to our knowledge, ever been recorded. Somehow, Fortune and Aminta made it from Virginia to Pennsylvania. Philadelphia was becoming known as the City of Brotherly Love as the Quakers gave up their slaves. It has been recorded that as early as 1688, four German Quakers in Germantown near Philadelphia protested slavery as 'traffic of Men-body' and believed that slavery was contrary to their religion.[40] By the late 1770s, abolitionism was a full-scale movement in the state.[41] We know that Fortune and Aminta ran away from William Bradley in Virginia and made it to Philadelphia by 1774, as that was the year and the place where their daughter Rose was born.[42] Author Ruth Holmes-Whitehead writes: "Enslaved people ....weren't given obituaries in the newspapers, but for those who made a bid for freedom, the runaway-slave advertisements surely serve as their memorials."[43]

Professor of history Andrew Diemer writes:

In 1765, of the approximately fifteen hundred black Philadelphians, all but about one hundred were enslaved. In the next few decades, though, this dramatically changed. The causes of this transformation were multiple. Some supporters of the revolutionary cause came to recognize a clear contradiction between their calls for liberty and the practice of slavery. Others, in particular some of Philadelphia's significant Quaker minority, grew to see slavery as a violation of deeply held religious beliefs .... By the end of the American Revolution, Philadelphia contained only four hundred slaves while its free black population had grown to over one thousand.[44]

With the constant resistance of the slaves by running away from their masters, things started to change in the northeast part of the Thirteen Colonies. 'Over time, these abolition laws, combined with the continuation of private manumissions of the Philadelphia region's remaining slaves, led to the growth of a free African-descended population, but a significant number of free Blacks also found their way to Philadelphia from elsewhere'.[45] Fortune and Aminta had come to Philadelphia from Virginia.

The runaway slave advertisement printed on page 37 in this book is very likely to be about Rose's parents. Although there were other enslaved people named Fortune in Virginia (I have come across at least two), the timing is wrong for the others. One of them was recorded as still being with his owner in 1787. His owner, Robert Sydnor of St. Martin's Parish, sub-contracted him out to another plantation owner in 1779. In 1780, it was recorded, amongst other slaves, as 'Fortune Returned'.[46] In 1787, this Fortune is recorded as being with another slave, 'Randolph', in Sydnor's *Memorandum of Negroes*.[47]

Then there is the story of the enslaved man named Fortune who lived in Waterbury, Connecticut. Fortune was owned by a bone surgeon, Dr. Porter. When Fortune died, Porter prepared Fortune's body to be stripped down to the skeleton and used for medical research in Dr. Porter's School for Anatomy.[48] In the early 20th century, Fortune's skeleton was donated to the Mattatuck Museum and has been used to study how Fortune lived and died.[49] It's a particularly interesting story, but this man was not our Fortune.

The runaway slave ad of April 29, 1773 has the right timing. According to family legend, Rose was born in 1774 outside of Philadelphia. This would have given fugitives Fortune and Aminta the time needed to run away from William Bradley in Virginia and make their way to free Black communities in and around Philadelphia, where Rose was born — either late in 1773 or in 1774. Although the fugitive slave records are not comprehensive, it is my belief, based on the description of Fortune and Aminta, on their parentage and on the DNA test results of three of Rose's descendants, that these fugitives were the parents of Rose Fortune.

There is no indication that Fortune, Aminta and Rose were enslaved in Pennsylvania, nor did they belong to a family named DeVone, Devon, Deveaux or any variation of that name. Instead, they most likely lived in a community outside of Philadelphia called Devon. Devon was, and is to this day, a hamlet in Chester County which was developed by the well-known Quaker William Penn in 1682. Devon had only one road going through it, the Conestoga Road, which connected Philadelphia with Lancaster.[50] One could see how, when recording names of people on passenger lists, it would be easy to make an erroneous stroke of the quill and accidently put down Devon as slave master instead of the village where they had lived.

A 1930s photograph of the Tea House in Devon, Pennsylvania. This building has been in Devon since 1734. Photo courtesy of Tredyffrin Easttown Historical Society.

Fortune and Aminta in Pennsylvania

When the Quakers first came to the New World in 1682, they brought their enslaved Africans with them. Increasingly, both the Quakers and the Presbyterians came to believe that slavery was a sin against God and slowly began manumitting their slaves. The New York slave revolt of 1712, in which 23 slaves rose up against their owners, killing nine of them and injuring six more, gave all slave owners a warning.[51] The white people of Pennsylvania, owning a significant population of slaves, might have taken heed of this revolt and begun to think about the implications of slavery. By 1726, the Quakers had passed a 'Black code' in Pennsylvania that required a £30 surety bond for freeing slaves, refused Blacks the right to inter-marry with whites and restricted the rights of Blacks, both free and enslaved, to travel, drink liquor and carry on trade.[52] After 1720, however, the peak of slavery had passed and more labour became available in the colony. More indentured and poor white Europeans immigrated to Pennsylvania, and white people in Philadelphia who needed cheap labour but wanted to avoid using slaves, now other had options.[53] Thus, slave-holding declined in the colony after the 1720s. In 1758, Quakers forbade all their members from importing or buying enslaved people.[54] Over the decades, slavery became less and less common in Pennsylvania. Historian and author J.R. Soderlund writes:

"By the 1770s even several slave owners who were affiliated with the Church of England, the religion most resistant in Philadelphia to anti-slavery reform, freed their slaves."[55]

Chester County, where the village of Devon is located, was Church of England. After manumitting their slaves, they allowed Black people to marry in their church. Did Fortune and Aminta formally marry here? Was this the reason why Rose and her family became followers of the Church of England? Some of Rose's descendants still are followers of this church.[56] The family history of Rose Fortune says that Rose was born in 1773 or 1774 outside of Philadelphia.[57] This could be the village of Devon. As Fortune and Aminta were considered free persons once they crossed into Pennsylvania and had no master, Rose would have been born a free person.

So how did Fortune and Aminta support themselves and Rose in Pennsylvania? Work for Fortune would likely have been either labour on a farm outside Philadelphia or manual labour within the city.[58] Historian Soderlund, who writes specifically about Chester County in Pennsylvania, where Devon is located, notes:

Black women continued to do domestic labor even after they were freed, working as servants and laundrywomen. In Chester County, most women also did housework, though here they would have tended larger gardens, raised poultry, milked cows, produced cloth, and helped in the fields (especially at harvest) as well.[59]

Fortune and Aminta probably worked much as they had when they were enslaved, except of course that they would now receive pay for their work. As Devon was not far from the city of Philadelphia (23 miles/37 kilometres), where a number of free Blacks also lived and worked, they would have had the support of other people in the same situation as themselves. Again, we turn to the words of Soderlund: "Philadelphia became the center of the black abolitionist movement of America after 1790 because already in the 1770s a relatively large and sophisticated free black population lived there."[60]

Some religious organizations decided not only to manumit their slaves, but to teach them to read and write before they gave them their freedom. Both the Quakers and the Church of England took on what they saw as a moral obligation to educate Blacks.[61] In Philadelphia, several schools were opened for Blacks.[62] They were referred to as 'African Schools'.[63] By the 1770s and 1780s, the Quaker committees reported back to their Society that most of the freed 'Negro' men and women were able to support themselves.[64]

What happened that made Fortune and Aminta decide to move to Nova Scotia along with so many Loyalists? They were free, their child was born free, education was available, work was available, a community of people similar to themselves was nearby for support and they could even own property.[65] Why would they want to move?

Despite rumours that suggest Fortune fought for the British in the American War of Independence, I could find no evidence to back that up. There are no records of Fortune in any of the Black Brigades or Black soldier rosters. Fortune was also quickly approaching what would have been considered old age for that time. He would have been in his late 40s or early 50s. Aminta was only 10 years younger, approaching 40 or in her early 40s. Rose, at the time of their decision to move to Nova Scotia, was only nine or ten years old.

Fortune, Aminta and Rose did not make it into the Book of Negroes, a list of African-descended people leaving New York for Nova Scotia. It has been noted, however, that the Book of Negroes did not include all of the Blacks who boarded the ships for Nova Scotia. Author Ruth Holmes-Whitehead argues in her book *Black Loyalists: Southern Settlers of Nova Scotia's First Free Black Communities* that the Book of Negroes and the muster rolls of the ships that carried the Freed Blacks to Nova Scotia have transcription errors. Names of some of the Freed and fugitive Blacks are recorded differently on the muster rolls, as compared to the Book of Negroes, with different spellings and genders. Some women and some children were reportedly recorded as being men.[66] To illustrate these errors Holmes-Whitehead gives us the story "Henry Middleton, sixteen, whose name is given as 'Minton' in the Book of Negroes, had been previously 'the property of Henry Middleton, Senior, Charlestown' for whom he may have been named."[67] It is not surprising that transcription mistakes were made. Is this why we don't see Fortune, Aminta and Rose in the Book of Negroes?

It is also possible that we do not see their names in the Book of Negroes because they were on a ship that did not have its Black passengers recorded. Holmes-Whitehead quotes the inspection of T. Gilfillan and William Armstrong, who, along with Messrs. Parker and Hopkins, working for the British, were to inspect those vessels embarking for Nova Scotia:

We also certify that bound to Nova Scotia excepting one Sloop and one Schooner which went off without being examined although ordered not to do it, but with which order they would not comply. We however sent a Message to Captain Henry Mowatt of His Majesty's ship La Sophia conveying the Fleet desiring him to bring back to this Place such Negroes or American Property as should be found in those vessels on their arrival in Nova Scotia.[68]

Note how the 'Negroes' are still referred to as 'American Property'. Did Rose and her parents make their way north from Philadelphia to the port of New York to board one of these ships bound for Nova Scotia?

One reason why Rose's family might have decided to leave Pennsylvania was the state of the economy at that time. Although free Blacks could work and receive a wage, the work became scarce and competitive. Historian Andrew Diemer writes:

One of the great draws of Philadelphia was the lure of economic opportunity. Newly emancipated African Americans from rural areas across the region and beyond saw promise in the burgeoning city. Once there, though, they often found that they were shunted into the lowest paying and least desirable kinds of work. This was compounded by the fact that Philadelphia was also a magnet for European immigration, creating fierce competition for low-wage work. While white workers found employment in the city's robust industrial sector, free Black people were largely excluded from this sort of work and relegated to employment as physical laborers in the low-status service economy.[69]

Another issue prompting the move to Nova Scotia could have been the location where Rose and her family lived in Pennsylvania. It bordered on Virginia, the slave-holding state where, as far as they knew, their last owner still lived. With the Colonies winning the War of Independence, it would be natural to fear that the slave-holding states would be given permission to retrieve their fugitive slaves in other states.

Perhaps the most urgent goal of free black communities, especially in regions like greater Philadelphia that bordered on slave states, was the protection of Black citizens from enslavement, kidnapping and white violence. Black communities were constantly on the lookout for those who generally claimed to be acting as legal slave catchers but who often were willing to kidnap the legally free as well.[70]

Although it happened nearly 90 years after Rose and her family left Pennsylvania, the narrative of Solomon Northup shows how this could and did happen. He was born a free man in New York City and was lured to Washington in 1841 on the promise of money. He was then kidnapped by slave catchers and spent over a decade as an enslaved man in Louisiana before escaping back to New York.[71] This scenario was a real possibility in Fortune and Aminta's time and thus may have influenced their decision to move to the British colony of Nova Scotia.

Certainly, Lord Dunmore's proclamation of November 7, 1775 would have tempted Fortune and Rose. It was issued off the coast of Virginia from a British warship by John Murray, royal governor of Virginia, Earl of Dunmore and Scottish aristocrat. In an attempt to counter an attack on Williamsburg by the patriot militia, Dunmore proclaimed that he would offer freedom to all slaves and indentured servants belonging to rebels and who were able to bear arms against the rebels. All the slaves and servants had to do was make it to British lines and they would be protected from their owners.[72] This was not a humanitarian effort toward enslaved Africans on the part of the British;

SLAVE-OWNER SHOOTING A FUGITIVE SLAVE.

A slave owner shooting at a fugitive slave. Note the dog chasing the fugitive as well. Etching by W.G. Mason, New York Public Library, Date Unknown, Wikimedia Commons.

rather, this was a direct attack on the slave-based economy of the rebels.[73] If the rebels could not receive an income from their plantations and businesses because they did not have slaves to do their work then, it was reasoned, they could not raise monies for the revolution against the British.

Many enslaved people had already run from their owners and made their way to more northern states, much as Fortune and Aminta had done, to Pennsylvania and free Black communities. For the enslaved and for the fugitives, the fight against America was a fight for their freedom. All they had to do was make it to the British lines:

> And Britain was as close as the nearest Royal Navy vessel, be it a man-of-war of the first rank or merely the tender to one of His Majesty's sloops. Britain was as close as the nearest detachment of British soldiers or the camp of any royal governor. It was as close as Nova Scotia or East Florida, still under British rule. After August 1776, it would become as close as New York, where the British would establish a command that lasted until the signing of the Treaty of Paris in 1783.[74]

Lord Dunmore, who 'had not one good quality to recommend him', did not have much in the way of sympathy for the enslaved men and women. He was unaffected by their sorrows, their treatment, their plight, even as they became his allies.[75] 'The slave population, he noted, was double that of its enslavers; the slaves had no ties of loyalty to their masters and could easily be persuaded, by any foreign power, to rise against them in return for promises of future freedom'.[76] And that is exactly what many Black slaves did.

Fortune, Aminta and their daughter Rose might have made their way to New York and from there, left with the British. Even though Fortune's name does not appear on any of the Black soldier musters, Fortune and Aminta could have assisted the British by doing physical labour or intelligence-gathering from the network of Blacks — enslaved, fugitive and free. Fortune and his family were already free, so they were not fighting for their freedom so much as to keep themselves and their neighbours free. When the British lost the war to the rebels, Blacks such as Fortune and his family were promised freedom in a British-controlled colony — one called Nova Scotia.

By *his Excellency the Right Honourable* JOHN *Earl of* DUNMORE, *his*

Majesty's Lieutenant and Governour-General of the Colony and Dominion of

Virginia, *and Vice-Admiral of the fame:*

A PROCLAMATION.

AS I have ever entertained Hopes that an Accommodation might have taken Place between *Great Britain* and this Colony, without being compelled, by my Duty, to this moft difagreeable, but now abfolutely neceffary Step, rendered fo by a Body of armed Men, unlawfully affembled, firing on his Majefty's Tenders, and the Formation of an Army, and that Army now on their March to attack his Majefty's Troops, and deftroy the well-difpofed Subjects of this Colony: To defeat fuch treafonable Purpofes, and that all fuch Traitors, and their Abetters, may be brought to Juftice, and that the Peace and good Order of this Colony may be again reftored, which the ordinary Courfe of the civil Law is unable to effect, I have thought fit to iffue this my Proclamation, hereby declaring, that until the aforefaid good Purpofes can be obtained, I do, in Virtue of the Power and Authority to me given, by his Majefty, determine to execute martial Law, and caufe the fame to be executed throughout this Colony; and to the End that Peace and good Order may the fooner be reftored, I do require every Perfon capable of bearing Arms to refort to his Majefty's S T A N- DARD, or be looked upon as Traitors to his Majefty's Crown and Govern- ment, and thereby become liable to the Penalty the Law inflicts upon fuch Offences, fuch as Forfeiture of Life, Confifcation of Lands, &c. &c. And I do hereby farther declare all indented Servants, Negroes, or others (appertaining to Rebels) free, that are able and willing to bear Arms, they joining his Majefty's Troops, as foon as may be, for the more fpeedily reducing this Colony to a proper Senfe of their Duty, to his Majefty's Crown and Dignity. I do farther order, and require, all his Majefty's liege Subjects to retain their Quitrents, or any other Taxes due, or that may become due, in their own Cuftody, till fuch Time as Peace may be again reftored to this at prefent moft unhappy Country, or demanded of them for their former falutary Purpofes, by Officers properly authorifed to receive the fame.

GIVEN under my Hand, on Board the Ship William, *off* Norfolk,

the 7th *Day of* November, *in the* 16th *Year of his Majefty's Reign.*

D U N M O R E.

G O D save the K I N G.

A Copy

Lord Dunmore's proclamation, dated June 7, 1775, offering freedom to any "Negroes who would rebel against their rebel masters".

CHAPTER 3

Life in Brinley Town

"We're here
Standing at the shoreline
Made it through some hard times
Black Mother, Black Daughter"
— song written by George Elliott Clarke, performed by Four the Moment - A Capella group for Sylvia Hamilton's documentary film *Black Mother, Black Daughter*

Rose was desperately upset. Her face was puffy and wet with tears. Fortune was dead. Rose and Aminta had tried desperately to save him but he became weaker and weaker as the weather became colder and colder. Finally, with Rose, Aminta and Joseph Leonard by his side, Fortune slipped away quietly in his sleep. Rose and her mother were alone in this new land. Their friends and neighbours from Philadelphia were either in Halifax or in the new Loyalist settlement of Shelburne. They knew no one here except the preacher, Leonard. What would they do? Where would they go?

Leonard said he would leave them with Fortune's body, to pray over him. He would come back with some men after they had dug a grave for Fortune and they would have a service over him. A few hours later, Rose and her mother, Leonard and the grave diggers and a handful of Negro people that neither Rose nor Aminta knew, gathered at Fortune's grave. They wrapped him in the old black quilt they had brought from Virginia and lowered him into the grave with ropes. The winds blew from the chilly northeast, warning of the impending winter and the sky was as grey and cold as the metal of a gun. The women sang keenly, old spirituals that spoke of sorrow in life and freedom in death. Rose tried to comfort herself with the words of these songs but, oh how she would miss her father. She and her mother felt adrift with no direction now that Fortune was gone. Rose wrapped her father's coat around her, not only to keep out the cold of the day but also to smell him and feel his arms encircling her.

They returned to their tent which, even though it was small, felt empty without Fortune's presence. He was no longer on the bed of fir boughs they had made for him; he was no longer sitting by the fire outside the tent when he was strong enough. Fortune was gone.

Rose and her mother were alone and must decide what to do. Her mother, when she did not have silent tears running down her face, would talk with herself: "Maybe we should go to our people in Birchtown," she said aloud. "But how will we get there? I haven't any money for us to eat, let alone for travelling. What direction do we go in? How will we survive? I don't know. I don't know," she cried, rocking and hugging herself in grief. Other women came by to comfort them, to offer them prayers and friendship through this awful time, but no one had any answers for them.

The answer soon came. Joseph Leonard entered their small tent that evening, bringing a pot of boiled tea and some biscuits made from acorns the women had ground into flour. The community had shared what little they had to help them through this grieving time. Rose and Aminta were not the only ones to lose a family member, but every woman knew what it would be like to lose their man, whether through death or re-enslavement. There would be no money, no one to help with raising the children, no one to build a hut for them, no one to protect them. The best thing that Aminta could do was find another man … and quickly. But that was the last thing she wanted right now.

Leonard sat on a blanket with them as Aminta poured the hot tea. Rose ate her biscuit quickly. She might be grieving but she was also hungry. Food was scarce in this new world.

"I have only told a few people this Aminta," he started. "A sergeant in the Black Pioneers, Thomas Peters and I will tell everyone tomorrow. We will call a meeting of everyone and announce the news. But I wanted to tell you quietly tonight so that you may sleep with a little peace."

Aminta and Rose waited expectantly for Leonard to tell them his news.

"Our people are moving to a new place," he told them. "Some Loyalists are going to be packing up boats soon and moving south, to the far side of this basin. They are forming a new town. There is a group of our people who are already outside this new town. You will have heard of the Black Pioneers who were with the British during the war. They have petitioned for land to settle on now that the war is over. Peters and I have petitioned with the town as well. We have all gotten permission from the government."

"We have our people here in this town," Aminta pointed out. "Are we just going to starve and freeze in a new place down the basin?"

Leonard shook his head. "The new place has plenty of forest all around it, not like here, where the forests have been cut back for miles. We'll have firewood and wood for making our homes. We're going to have a school just for our children and a church for our followers. Peters has been promised that he can have a church for his followers as well. The government has promised the Black Pioneers land grants and provisions of food. We can farm the land and have plenty to eat and our own community."

Rose watched her mother, silent, thinking about it. Rose quietly hoped that her mother would like the idea; it seemed better than this place where every nook and cranny was filled with people who were cold and hungry like them. And the local white preacher, Reverend Bailey, wouldn't help them. He already had too many poor Loyalists to help and the rich Loyalists even complained about that. They sure weren't going to let Reverend Bailey help out any poor Negro folk, even if they were followers of the Church of England. Rose didn't want to go over any large bodies of water to some other place that was unknown to them or travel through miles and miles of forest to get to Birchtown, on the other side of the province where Shelburne was being built. The word was filtering through from other travellers that their people in Birchtown were also having a hard time.

"How many of our people are going with you?" Aminta asked.

"More than 100," Leonard answered. "A few white folks put some money together and hired some boats to take all of us to our new settlement. We'll even take our tents and huts with us. Everyone will share everything we have until we get our land grants and get our farms set up."

"Mister Leonard!" a male voice shouted from outside their tent. "Sorry to interrupt but I got some good news"

"What is it, my son?" Leonard asked.

"Me and Pomp just shot and killed a big fat caribou. And Moses returned with news from Birchtown and brought a brace of rabbits he killed on the way back. The women are cleaning everything now to cook 'em."

"That is indeed good news," Leonard answered. "I'll be over momentarily."

Turning back to Rose and Aminta he said: "It looks as though we'll sup well for the next two days."

"We'll go with you to this new settlement," Aminta said abruptly. "And me and Rose will go help the women right now."

"And maybe," Aminta muttered to herself, practical now, "I'll find a new man. I'll miss Fortune but Rose and I need to have a man to protect us. And a man needs a woman to keep his home warm and his meals cooked. And all of us need to help each other."

The move to this new settlement outside the Loyalist town that was first named Conway and then Digby, after Admiral Digby, took several days and many boat trips. Some loaded onto ships with the white folks for the short trip down the basin; others travelled through the woods over rocks and through bogs for two days to reach the new town. Some of their people decided to stay in the Annapolis Royal area and they eventually made their own settlements in Granville Ferry, Thorne's Cove, Delaps Cove, Lequille and other places. But most of the Black folk in Annapolis came with Peters and Leonard to this new settlement.

While they waited for the government to organize land grants for the Black Pioneers, the Black settlers immediately began the work of clearing the forest. It quickly became apparent that the soil was not suitable for farming; however the land was located next to excellent fishing grounds. Those who had huts in Annapolis Royal dismantled them and brought them to this new settlement, named Brinley Town. Thomas Peters, Joseph Leonard and other leaders of the people decided to name their new settlement after a sympathetic Loyalist, George Brinley, who was then in Halifax. By the turn of the next century, people would come to call it Negro Town or Little Joggin.

The people built new huts, gathered firewood and hunted for food. As their land was situated at the shores of what became known as the Little Joggin Cove, they also fished and clammed and picked lobsters to eat. Over the winter they huddled together from the cold, collecting driftwood from the shores of the Annapolis Basin. The wood was often so embedded with dried salt that it snapped and sputtered with noises and flames of blue and red. Around these flames of warmth, the Black settlers of Brinley Town swapped life stories of what they had been through in slavery, in running away, of being fugitives. The favourite stories were those that were told by the Africans who

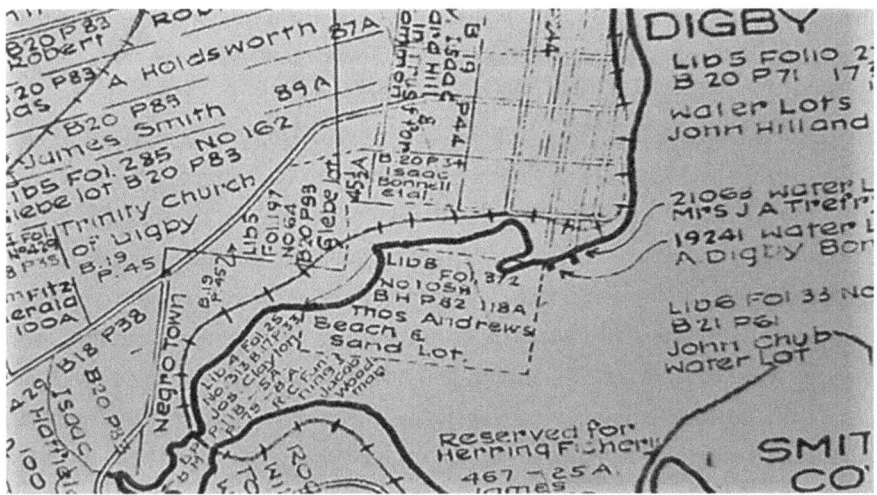

Department of Natural Resources Map 1900 showing "Negro Town," where Brinley Town once stood

had been born, lived and kidnapped in Africa, sold in America and escaped to Nova Scotia. They told the former slaves and free Blacks shivering around the driftwood fires of life in Africa - of warmth and the green of the jungles, of villages and their families. The people of Brinley Town wore their clothes to bed and huddled from the cold under their coats, sharing their body warmth and dreaming of Africa. They shared what food they had and what strength they had and made it through to spring. Some of them died; especially the sick, the old and some babies, but most of them made it through.

And Aminta found a new man. It was not difficult. Men needed women as much as women needed men and each had their duties for day-to-day survival. Women cleaned what the men hunted and fished, cooked it with any wild herbs and plants that they could find, kept the huts warm when the men came in from the cold, raised the children to be good Christians and strong workers who were obedient to their elders. They did this in exchange for food and protection and even, often,..... love. When her new man Michael built himself a hut in the spring, Aminta and Rose moved in with him. The task of living and getting on with life, after grief, commenced.

The first two years were spent building their hut bigger, making room for neighbours who needed shelter, harvesting food, putting a kitchen garden in the sandy soil to try and grow some root vegetables to keep them through the winter. Gathering wood, hunting and fishing for food, smoking their fish to preserve it, collecting salt from the ocean to preserve moose and caribou meat, and gathering together with neighbours to worship and plan the building of their churches kept everyone busy. Rose and Aminta worked at all these things and stored food away; they never wanted to be hungry like they were that first winter of 1784. It turned out they were wise to do this. By 1787, things were changing. A famine came upon the land. No one knew what had caused the famine; however, Rose's small family of three made it through that first year. Everyone had been expecting, hoping for a better year in 1788, but this was not to be. The famine raged on. Rose and her mother were having a difficult time getting anything but weeds to grow in their little garden on their one acre plot. Michael was coming home with meat less and less frequently and the fish had migrated someplace else. The moose and caribou were being over-hunted, with all these new settlers on the land. Rabbits and clams saved their family through the famine. Aminta and Rose even boiled down the bones of the rabbits and the shells of the clams to make a broth to get them through times where they didn't have anything to eat.

Surely, they thought, this will be over by the next year, 1789. It was not to be. For the third year the famine swept through most of the province and many people died from starvation. Rose's family saw their neighbours killing and eating their cats and dogs in sheer desperation. Aminta had sold just about everything of value that they had. She sold off much of what they had brought with them from Virginia, but Rose begged her not to sell Fortune's brown coat and hat. Rose was sure she could still smell her father in the depths of that coat. Her mother's new man was okay, but he wasn't her father. Aminta relented and let Rose keep Fortune's coat and brimmed hat.

After Sunday worship at the church, the congregation members often gathered to talk about this new settlement. What food that was being given out was going to the white folk first. The Black folk did receive 80 days' worth of basic food rations, but that was it. And the people of Brinley Town knew that until the white folks got their land, there was not a chance of them buying or receiving any land of their own.

"We coulda had a farm started and had some crops stored if we had got our lands by now," they grumbled.

"On this soil?" argued others. "This soil isn't fit to raise pigs on."

They all agreed that this was not the Promised Land. Some of them had been given one acre and no more. How could they live off that?

They were hearing word from Birchtown, outside of Shelburne, that the famine was bad there as well. One of the leaders of the Black Pioneers, Thomas Peters, who had been born in Nigeria, brought to the Thirteen Colonies as a slave and was now a free man in Nova Scotia, decided that

Thomas Peters, artist unknown.

something had to be done to improve their situation. Peters started a petition which he took to the residents of Birchtown, Brinley Town and Saint John, and people signed it or gave their mark. The petition stated that the Black Pioneers and the Negro settlers had not been given their provisions and that they would kindly like this to be rectified as soon as possible. If the white people in the colony weren't helping the Black Pioneers, maybe the British Government would be a bit more helpful and speed this thing along. By 1790, plans were completed to send Thomas Peters to England to speak at Whitehall, seat of the English government.

Brinley Town - A Free Black Community

Family legend passed down by generations of descendants of Rose Fortune states that Fortune died shortly after arriving in Annapolis. It certainly would explain why we don't see any further mention of him in either muster rolls or censuses that were taken in the area after their arrival. As Rose and her mother either moved in with another family or Aminta took up with another man, they would have disappeared from historical records. Recorded history has been based on the experiences of white men in positions of power[77] Uncovering the experiences of white women can be difficult; finding the experiences of Black women is often impossible. Historian Dr. J.A. Mannette writes:

It is a difficult task to make women of subordinate groups visible, especially Black women, inferior and unimportant as they were and are seen to be in the wider society ... Fox-Genovese points out that social theory's response to gender analysis has been an impoverished inclusion as "other" which renders women, as historical subjects, invisible. Further, she explicitly acknowledges the deficit in "women's history" of theorising about and analyses of Black women.[78]

Historian Suzanne Morton also notes that documents that record the history of Black women are scarce and biased:

Research on African-Nova Scotians in the 19th century is generally hampered by the paucity of reliable sources. Descriptions by Nova Scotians of European descent are marked by racism and by a disregard that extended to government records such as the decimal census.[79]

The decimal census that Morton refers to is the system used in the 18th century when the Loyalists arrived in Nova Scotia. The 'heads of families' — men — were recorded by name and often occupation. The women and children who were attached to the men were recorded with a slash under a column separating them as 'Women' and 'Children'. Sometimes the children were recorded as under a certain age or over a certain age but women and children's names were not recorded. Thus, they became invisible to history. Fortune was recorded in the muster roll of 1784 and we can only assume that Rose was the ten-year-old child recorded as being with him.[80]

We lost the name of Aminta, the mother of Rose and wife of Fortune, until the runaway slave ad was found. We knew she existed, but we did not know her name for 224 years! And even now, we cannot help but wonder if her name was spelled accurately or if it was a misspelling of another name. The name Aminta is Greek and means 'defender'. Aminata, which I believe was her real name, is Swahili and means 'serenity'.[81] Aminata Diallo was the name of the central character of Lawrence Hill's stunning book *The Book of Negroes*.[82] For the purpose of this book, however, we shall follow what she is named on primary-source documents.

It is not certain that Rose and her mother moved to Brinley Town, which

This excerpt from the muster roll of discharged officers, disbanded soldiers and Loyalists taken in Annapolis County 18-24 June 1784 almost certainly refers to the family of Rose Fortune (ca 1774–1864). Fortune is the sixth one down and the listing shows how women and children were lost in the decimal system of census taking of the time.

is often mis-spelled itself with a "d" added to make it Brindley Town. As I discuss in Appendix 1, evidence that has been uncovered points to them moving to Brinley Town. Some historians of Rose Fortune disagree with me and believe she may have been in the Black community outside of Liverpool; others think she moved to Saint John, New Brunswick, which was still a part of Nova Scotia in those days. Checking the records of both Birchtown (Shelburne County) and Saint John, there is no evidence of the presence of either Rose or Aminta. They do not appear outside of Liverpool or Parrsboro either. However, they could have been lost to the decimal census system, as mentioned earlier. Until further evidence is revealed, the location of Rose during the years 1785 to 1828 will remain a mystery.

If Aminta was still alive, she would have needed to find a partner as soon as possible to ensure their survival. I have imagined a gendered division of labour within and outside the household, as this was the standard of the 18th

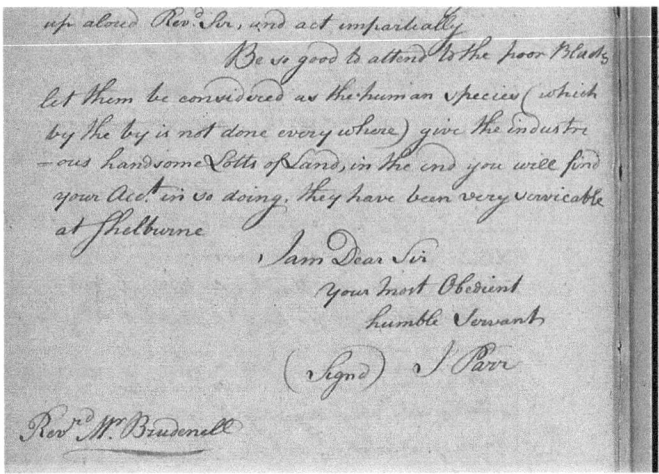

up aloud Revᵈ Sir, and act impartially

Be so good to attend to the poor Blacks let them be considered as the human species (which by the by is not done every where) give the industri—ous handsome Lotts of Land, in the end you will find your Acct in so doing, they have been very serviceable at Shelburne

I am Dear Sir

Your most Obedient humble Servant,

(Signd) J Parr

Revᵈ Mr Brudenell

Letter, undated, from Governor Parr, to Rev. Edward Brudenell, an agent for the British government in settling the Loyalists in Digby Township. The letter was regarding the treatment of the "poor Blacks" at Brinley Town, Brudenell Letter Book, Harvard University, sequence 50.

through to the 20th centuries. Whitfield writes about the importance of finding a partner in his book *North to Bondage, Loyalist Slavery in the Maritimes:*

> Rural slaves were relatively isolated, with little chance to form families or communities, whereas those in Annapolis could potentially live near family members, find marriage partners, and form a community. Moreover, there were significant numbers of free blacks in Annapolis, who offered opportunities for socializing and possibly running away.[83]

The same could be said of the free Blacks. As there were more free Blacks in Annapolis and Shelburne Counties, there would be more opportunity to find a partner in a community of people like themselves. Although slavery in Nova Scotia was never as concentrated as it was in the United States, particularly in the south, it still existed and there was still a threat of re-enslavement to free Blacks. 'Slavery existed in most parts of the colony but was particularly strong in Shelburne and the Annapolis region.'[84] It is important to remember that Annapolis County at that time included Digby and surrounding areas.

Digby did not have as many slave-holders as Annapolis Royal and its surrounding areas; however, there were still slave-holders there. The presence of free Black people in numbers would not only have had an impact on the enslaved Blacks, who might consider running away to be free themselves (which some did, escaping to free Black communities and being taken under their protection[85]), it could be argued that it would also have dissuaded white people from attempting to re-enslave anyone of the Black population for fear of reprisals. However, the courts showed the free Black people and in particular, the fugitive slaves, that this was not the case.

The Story of Mary Postell

dusty brown potato
white eyes protruding
she turns it in
her hand, knife poised
and thinks
of Mary Postill
sold
for a bushel of potatoes
    —Sylvia Hamilton "Potato Lady"

The story of Mary Postell of Shelburne showed the Black population how tenuous their freedom was. Mary Postell (also spelled Postill) went to court in 1791 and, as sad as her story was, gives us insight into the way free Black people of Nova Scotia were treated, not only by white people but also by the Loyalist courts.

Postell had been born enslaved and was owned by a South Carolina planter when the American Revolutionary War began. A wise woman, she took advantage of Lord Dunmore's proclamation and managed to get herself, her husband and her daughter Flora behind British lines, thus claiming her family's freedom. She was given a much-needed certificate of freedom. This valuable piece of paper, however, was taken away from her by a white person who pretended they wanted to see it and then kept it. Unfortunately, this kind of incident happened all too often with free Blacks.[86] The lack of a certificate of freedom made Mary and her family vulnerable to re-enslavement. A white person, Jesse Gray, promised to get them to freedom in Spanish-held Florida if they signed up as his indentured servants. Mary signed up herself and her daughter and Gray got them to St. Augustine, Florida. Once there, however, Gray claimed Mary and Flora as his slaves and then sold Mary to his brother Samuel. At some point during her two years of enslavement with Samuel, Mary had another daughter, Nell.

During the evacuation of Florida, the two brothers emigrated to Nova Scotia with the Loyalists, taking Mary and her daughters with them. Samuel sold Mary back to his brother Jesse, and they settled in Shelburne. Mary became anxious that Gray would sell her again or sell her daughters. Her fears were well founded. In 1790, Gray sold her daughter Flora to John Henderson for £5. Henderson then took the child to South Carolina. Fearful that Gray would do this to her other daughter, Mary and Nell ran away from Gray, escaping to Birchtown. Here she fought back against their enslavement by taking Jesse Gray to court. What followed was an extraordinary and sad case in Nova Scotia's history.

Mary made a complaint against Jesse Gray in an attempt not only to ensure their freedom, but to protect her daughter Nell and possibly to get her daughter Flora back. In her complaint again Jesse Gray of Argyle, Postell claims that Gray violated the 'King's Peace' by enslaving them in St. Augustine and again in Shelburne. 'Gray, the indictment continued, through a combination of 'grievous threatenings and other enormous abuses [did] compel, terrify and oblige [the three] to serve, Work, and Labour' for his profit'.[87]

R. v. Gray (indictment of Jesse Gray for selling Mary Postell as a slave and kidnapping Flora Postell, her daughter) Nova Scotia Archives.

Postell argued that she and her children were free Blacks and that Jesse Gray had no right to enslave or sell them. To support her claim, friends of Mary's from Birchtown (which was also known as Black Town) testified in court on her behalf. Scipio and Dinah Waring (their names are spelled 'Wearing' in Nova Scotian court records) had been neighbouring slaves in South Carolina of Mary Postell and were related by marriage. They testified that Mary had only ever belonged to the Postell family of South Carolina and that Mary had run away from her owner and worked behind British lines, thus earning a certificate of freedom for herself and her daughter Flora. Her daughter Nell, she argued, was born a free Black.

In his defence, Jesse Gray claimed he bought Mary and her child Flora from Joseph Rea (or Wray) of Virginia while he was in St. Augustine in 1783. He brought forth a few witnesses but claimed he had lost his original receipt.

Tragically, while Scipio and Dinah were testifying in Mary's defence, a group of men set their house on fire. The fire killed one of Scipio and Dinah's children, who was in the house when it burnt down; thus, the men had committed murder.

The court found Jesse Gray not guilty. It ruled that Mary Postell was still considered a slave, as were her daughters. In retaliation, it is assumed, for her audacity of taking him to court, Gray sold Mary Postell to William Mangham for 'One Hundred Bushels of Potatoes'.[88]

The Threat of Re-enslavement

The Postell case made the following message perfectly clear to free Blacks and any Black slave willing to escape their master: *Your freedom is precarious.* The presence of slave-owners and slaves made free Black people nervous, as their colour alone associated them with slavery and made them susceptible to re-enslavement.[89] Whitfield writes:

One of the most fascinating aspects about slavery is that it opens up questions about the contours of Black Loyalist freedom. Indeed, as the primary source documents indicate, the difference between free and enslaved Blacks was remarkably fluid. The primary sources show the type of ambiguity that Black people, slave or free, encountered on a daily basis.[90]

Indeed, famous Nova Scotian historian and 'friend' of Rose Fortune, Thomas Chandler Haliburton, contributed to this discourse on re-enslavement by suggesting the Black settlers were miserable and a drain on society when he wrote in his famous series of stories of Sam Slick:

> At Preston and at Hammond Plains, in the neighbourhood of Halifax, there were settlements, composed wholly of Blacks, who experienced every winter all the misery incident to indolence and improvidence, and levied heavy contributions on the humanity of their more frugal neighbours. In some instances they have sighed for the roof of their master, and the pastimes and amusements they left behind.[91]

Pastimes and amusements? Sighed for the roof of their master? Haliburton clearly had a white Eurocentric view of slavery and had never considered what it must be like to be Black and poor in Nova Scotia! Haliburton put the plight of the African-Nova Scotians on their own shoulders, without taking into consideration the systemic racism that the white culture perpetuated — both then and now.

The freedom of so many Black people caused problems not only for the slave-owners but also for the slaves. Historian James W. St. G. Walker writes in his 1976 ground-breaking book *The Black Loyalists*:

> The Presence of so many free Blacks in Nova Scotia after 1783 naturally presented a problem to slave owners. With slave and free mingling in schools and markets it was difficult to maintain the notion in the slave's own mind, that he deserved to be in servitude because of his colour. It was equally difficult for whites to identify a wandering Black as a runaway, since a Black face could no longer be assumed to be a badge of bondage.[92]

Whitfield notes in his article 'The Struggle Over Slavery in Maritime Colonies' that "the place of Black people, slave or free, remained quite clear. Slaves and free Blacks were regularly reminded that they belonged on the lowest level of society, or indeed outside of society altogether."[93] Black communities were often located outside of white towns, cities and settlements. Birchtown (of which there were many much smaller Birchtowns in the province) was located outside of Shelburne, Lequille was outside of Annapolis Royal, Inglewood was outside of Bridgetown, the Black settlement in Granville Ferry was a kilometre behind the village and Brinley Town was three kilometres outside the town of Digby. Historian and author Barry Moody writes:

> Most of the newly arrived free Blacks who settled in the Annapolis area did so not in the town itself but in what evolved into the community of Lequille, just south of the town. There is no indication that they were forbidden to live within the town proper, and in fact some families did, but the houses and lots available for purchase or rent within the town were beyond the means of most of these former slaves, and more expensive than even many poorer white Loyalists could afford.[94]

Historians of the Loyalists agree that the hardships faced by Rose and Aminta and the Black settlers and slaves of Annapolis County were also felt by the Loyalists. The Loyalists faced a lack of proper housing, food shortages and lack of promised provisions. Walker writes: "A Digby petition claimed that the whites there had received no rations at all in 1784.... Clearly, the Blacks had no monopoly on poverty and unfulfilled promises."[95] The Loyalists, depending upon their class when they arrived in Annapolis, clearly suffered.

Every available building in Annapolis, including the church, was used for shelter, yet hundreds of people remained without a roof. Some of the more fortunate families there had "a single apartment built with sods, where men, women, children, pigs, fleas, bugs, mosquitoes and other domestic insects, mingle in society."[96]

However, Loyalists had the advantage over the Blacks in that they could decide to go back south to the United States. Moody makes this point:

> Although a number of white Loyalists ... would later quietly return to the United States when opportunity offered, such an option was not open to the Black settlers, however poorly they were treated, and no matter how destitute they became in this new "Promised Land." Re-enslavement would have been the least of their punishments if they had returned to the United States.[97]

Returning to the lands they were most familiar with was not an option for Black people in 18th and 19th-century Nova Scotia. Re-enslavement and death would have been there to greet them.

The Famine of 1787-1789

Rose and Aminta, wherever they were at the time in Nova Scotia, would have lived through the famine of 1787–1789. It was severe across Nova Scotia, with many people dying of starvation. To ward off such a death, people sold what belongings they had to purchase food. 'The conditions of famine in 1789 ... naturally struck hardest at the Black people'.[98] Some Blacks sold themselves as indentured servants or indentured their family members. Others sold themselves as slaves.[99] Some Blacks made their way to Halifax seeking employment. Even if jobs were available, Blacks were paid less than whites. This created racial tension, as the Blacks were willing to work for a quarter of what white people were paid and the employers, looking to save money for themselves, would hire the Black workers over the white workers.[100]

The suffering of the Black people in Brinley Town in 1788 was noted by Major Milledge in Digby:

Never was distress more apparent than amongst these poor people many of whom are almost without Clothing. Numbers of whom I fear are destitute of the necessaries of Life and before the end of the ensuing Winter will feel the most keen Distress.[101]

Walker writes of the charity of white people that saved many Blacks from cold and starvation. David George of Birchtown, Shelburne County had received a bag of seed potatoes from a white Baptist family named Taylor. George planted the seed potatoes and from that bag, harvested a crop of 35 bushels of potatoes, which saved his family and his extended family.

At Brindley Town it was only "by the Humanity of the White People that several of those helpless Black people exist." It was the Associates of the late Dr. Bray, a London-based Anglican charity particularly concerned for Black people in America that did most in an organised way to assist the destitute "Black Loyalists". To Birchtown they sent boxes of blankets, clothing and shoes in 1787 and again in 1789. Digby likewise received shoes and clothing and material with which to make their own clothes, including thread, buttons and patterns.[102]

It was also during this famine that some white families, unable to afford food for their own family members, turned out their Black slaves, giving them 'freedom'.[103] The newly freed slaves, used to taking directions without question and living their lives under constant watch, fear and threats in many cases, were now to find some fire of resourcefulness within to save themselves and their families. Many made their way to free Black communities. 'Birchtown became a haven to which slaves from all over the province could flee, and once safely hidden there it was extremely unlikely that a master could retrieve them'.[104]

How did Rose and Aminta survive the famine of 1787–1789? It is my theory that Aminta found a new partner in Brinley Town. The muster roll of 1784 for Digby certainly shows several single men. Their homes were likely built of wood and sod. There is no record of them building pit houses as the Black community of Birchtown did. Although the Black Pioneers of Brinley Town had not yet been given their land grants from the government, the community made the decision to settle on land referred to as the Little Joggin on the shores of the Annapolis Basin, a grant that eventually was given to a Loyalist named McKenny. Thomas Milledge, writing to Governor Parr in Halifax in 1785 notes:

> The benevolent disposition your Excellence provides emboldens me to lay before him a few facts for your Excellency's consideration. The Negroes have been in a very unsettled state at their place, until last summer having built Hutts at some expense on one McKennys land, not having until the above time lands assigned them. Several of these people have now built themselves comfortable Hutts in which they live. Cleared, joined land and made themselves gardens and of suffered to enjoy the lands they are now in possession and may be in a likely way with industry to make themselves a comfortable living. Their Town is about a mile from the upper part of the Town of Digby adjoining what is called the little Joggin; a place convenient to keep small fishing craft in, it being of great importance that these people have access or Plan thereof is delivered to the Surveyor General, having understood from

them that it was your Excellency's intention that in their town they should have lots of that quantity.

The lands for the Black Pioneers will be surveyed as soon as the snow admits of traveling to do it and I wish that their land also might be as contagious [illegible].

There is talk in this place that wishes to remove these people to some other place; in that case they must begin anew, with much cost and expense, which they are not able to undergo. I do not believe they have Five Pounds to move with; if they are obliged to move nothing but the utmost distress will be the consequence. On the other hand, if they are suffered to enjoy the lands are now in possession of there is a probability of their doing well. As the Negroes are now in this country the principles of Humanity dictate that to make them useful to them-selves as well as Society is to give them a good chance to live, and not to destroy them.

Thus, I have endeavoured to give your Excellency a true state of the case of those Negroes amongst us and should it meet your appro-bation to continue them where they are, I should think my time well spent. I am actuated by no other motive than that of Humanity.

I have the Honor to be with the greatest respect a true copy of the one in my hand

Thomas Milledge[105]

Regardless of the 'comfortable hutts' mentioned by Milledge, 'the only heat for these makeshift homes came from green wood the Black settlers cut and split. Some built crude chimneys out of mud and fieldstones; others simply lived with the smoke'.[106] Could Rose and Aminta have been in one of those huts with Aminta's new partner? From their location in Brinley Town, they could look across the cove to see the upper parts of the new Loyalist town of Digby being built. They could look directly across the Annapolis Basin and see ships coming from the Bay of Fundy through the Digby Gut, which the Mi'kmaq called Tee-wee-den, translated to 'Little Hole'. They had easy access to fishing in the basin and in the Bay of Fundy. The shore-line they were on meant access to clams, mussels, lobsters and shore fish. This must have helped Rose's family survive the famine years. The crustaceans could be gathered and not only eaten but sold to the local Loyalists.

Did Aminta and Rose become domestic servants to the Loyalists in Digby and area to survive? I can find no record of this. There is no written or pictorial evidence that Rose suffered from the effects of childhood malnutrition in adulthood. No written records of her mention that she had skeletal deformities, which could have been brought on by rickets and no mention of the loss of her permanent teeth, brought on by scurvy. Rose's short stature could be a result of childhood malnutrition or genetics (Aminta's height was recorded as 'small'), or a combination of both.

The Importance of the Church to Rose

The Church would have been an extremely important component for the survival of not only Rose and Aminta, but also their Brinley Town neighbours. Walker writes: "As slaves in the American colonies they had been discouraged, and sometimes even prevented, from embracing the religion of their owners."[107] In their new liberty, however, many Blacks looked to religion for themselves and their families for community support, for faith, for ease of anxiety and depression, for relationships and hope for the future. "They daily crowd to me for Baptism and seem happy with their prospects of Religion and Freedom," one Halifax rector recorded.[108] Other rectors across the province noted the same thing. If Rose and her parents did spend ten years in Devon, Pennsylvania, the predominant religion in that area was the Church of England. This church not only allowed — reluctantly at first — Blacks to join their congregation, they even performed marriages for Blacks.[109]

The Loyalists of Annapolis Royal and area were predominantly Church of England congregants.[110] 'Owing to the vigilance of the Magistrates, proponents of Nonconformist sects were restricted in their movements around Annapolis'.[111] These non-conformists sects included the New Lights and Methodists.

The churches were also interested in the affairs of the newly arrived Blacks. Walker records that the Archbishop of Canterbury wrote to Bishop Inglis to inquire how the Blacks were faring as free settlers. Inglis, while not an abolitionist, did offer spiritual guidance and importantly, supported education for Blacks.[112] This concern for the spiritual needs of the newly arrived Blacks did

Cornerstone of the Trinity Church of Digby, 1788. Photo courtesy of waymarking.com.

not mean that Black people were accepted as equals to the white; they were not permitted to mingle with the white parishioners.

A special gallery was fitted in St. Paul's church (Halifax) in 1784, to which the Blacks were confined "during divine service." But the huge number of Loyalist Anglicans made too great a demand on the limited space available, and it became impossible to admit all those wishing to attend of a Sunday. The Blacks, therefore, were excluded, and as an alternative the rector advised them to gather in private homes and he commissioned "several capable Negroes who read the Instructions to the Negroes and other pious Books" to as many of them as assemble for that purpose.[113]

A similar situation was experienced by Black people in other denominations. In Brinley Town, however, the number of Black Anglicans outnumbered the white Anglicans.

When the Reverend Roger Viets arrived in 1786 to his new church in Digby, he found that of the 49 regular communicants, 31 of them were Black.[114] This changed over the course of a few years, and the Blacks turned from Viets' church to the preaching of Joseph Leonard in Brinley Town.

Joseph Leonard comes to our attention as one of the leaders of Brinley Town. Leonard worked with Thomas Peters in organizing the Black settlers within Brinley Town and other Black settlements.[115] As the Blacks met in private homes for worship and service, they chose Joseph Leonard from amongst their number to be instructed in Christian doctrines to meet the spiritual needs of his community.[116] Leonard was literate and took his duty seriously. Not only did he lead services of worship for his community, he took to baptizing their children and new converts to the sect, marrying couples, performing burial rites and administrating communions.[117] Bishop Inglis, during a visit to Digby, was shocked to learn of Leonard's actions as Leonard was not an ordained minister. Leonard immediately requested Bishop Inglis to ordain him as he stated that he and his flock wished 'to be entirely independent and separate from the whites, and to have a church of their own'.[118] This, of course, Inglis denied immediately, suggesting that the Blacks and Leonard should regularly attend the church in Digby.

The Digital Collection of Canada, on its website about Black Loyalists, notes the following about Joseph Leonard:

He [Joseph Leonard] spearheaded land petitions and served as the spokesman to the white community. Leonard also served as the Anglican lay preacher at Brindley Town, where his independence brought him into conflict with the white establishment. Leonard had been authorized to read from the bible and lead prayers, but he went well beyond that. He performed marriages, baptisms, and communion without having been ordained as a preacher. Eventually, this came to attention of Charles Inglis, the Bishop of Nova Scotia. Inglis traveled to Digby and confronted Leonard, who displayed no guilt, but only expressed his wish to be ordained as an Anglican minister. Inglis rejected him on the spot.[119]

The Black community wanted a church of their own and this was understandable. If they went to a white church, they could only attend if there was room for them. Even when there was room, they were physically separated from the general congregation and not permitted to associate with the white people. If they were already meeting in their own homes, in their own communities, separate from the whites, why couldn't they have their own church? Why couldn't they have their own ministers, preachers or priests? This treatment of African-Nova Scotians may have inadvertently promoted independent Black churches. 'The Baptists by intent, the Huntingtonians by coincidence, the Methodists and Anglicans by default, all created what were in effect independent Black branches only loosely tied or, in the first instance, completely untied, to any white hierarchy'.[120]

Unfulfilled Promises

The situation of land grants promised to both the white Loyalists and the Black Pioneers continued to be a case of negligence and possible corruption. Petitions and letters criss-crossed the province to the sitting governor in Halifax and back again in an attempt to sort the land grant system out. Meanwhile, although Thomas Milledge had requested that the Black settlers be permitted to stay on the land grant of the absentee McKenny, plans were being made to move them to another location which was surveyed and had plots laid over 467 acres. Milledge was then informed that this land was not for the Black Pioneers, but rather for a church and glebe land and he was to find another place to settle the Black Pioneers of Brinley Town.[121]

By 1788 Joseph Leonard had approached the governor with a request for land for himself and other Blacks who were subsisting on their 76 one-acre grants of land at Brinley Town. After much confusion and wrangling, a certificate for a tract of land was deeded in the area called Clements in September 1789. The surveying of lots of 50 acres, with a grant of 100 acres for Joseph Leonard, was given the green light to begin. Despite suffering after effects of the famine, the Black settlers cleared a road to their tract of land. And then everything stopped.[122]

According to Walker, it is not known why the Black settlers of Brinley Town stopped developing their land. Were they suspicious of having their land grants moved yet again? Did they wish to wait for a final confirmation of their land grants? The land in Clements sat mostly unoccupied, however in 1793, Viets records doing a baptism: 'Clements 14th October 1793 a Black child of Aesop Moses named Moses'.[123] Some of the Blacks did 'squat upon the land in the township and the rounds of petitions for land there began again, which finally brought them title to the land in November 1830'.[124] Meanwhile, the

Black settlers of Brinley Town in the 1780s and 1790s remained on the only land legally deeded to any of them; the 76 one-acre parcels on the shores of the Annapolis Basin outside the town of Digby.[125]

Try as they might to survive off fish, game and the gardens of their small plots, the Black settlers still needed promised rations from the government, as did the white settlers. When the disbanded Black Pioneers first arrived in Digby Township in May 1784, they began setting up their homesteads and counting on the rations to come from the British government. Walker writes: 'Digby Commissary Thomas Williams eventually issued 12,096 pounds of flour and 9,352 pounds of pork, representing 80 days full rations for 160 Black adults and 26 children'.[126] However, these rations were not given out until December of 1784 and as Williams wrote bluntly, 'it is all they are to git for the winter'.[127] As most Nova Scotians know, the winter is more than 80 days long and the growing and harvest season is well beyond the 80 days of rations. Walker also writes that even though Thomas Peters was to have taken delivery of these rations, they were stored in the cellar of Richard Hill on the orders of the Reverend Edward Brudenell, who was in charge of settling the Loyalists of Digby. Brudenell had the rations given out 'only to those Blacks who performed work on the township's roads'.[128] With no other means of support, the Black settlers who were able to do so worked on the roads in return for their rations. Of the 12,096 pounds of flour, 11,980 were given out. Of the 9,352 pounds of pork, 9,209 were given out. They did not even receive all their rations! Walker writes:

> No further supplies were ever given out. The Digby Blacks, therefore, received provisions only for a few months, not for the three years they had a right to expect, and for these they were forced to work. This labour requirement was not a condition placed on white Loyalists in Digby in order to receive their government support.[129]

Even then it may be assumed that their rations would have been inferior to the rations of the white settlers. In Preston, outside of Halifax, white Loyalist rations consisted of codfish, molasses, hard biscuit and occasionally meat. The Black population was given meal (usually a ground corn or wheat) and molasses.[130]

How did the Black settlers survive the famine of 1787–1789? Those who lived near the water, such as in Birchtown (Shelburne County) and Brinley Town, could supplement their small gardens with fish and crustaceans from the sea. Some, who were incapable or unprepared for the life of a farmer, might have offered themselves up as day labourers or domestic servants in the local towns.[131]

The Black workers, however, were not paid as much as the white workers and, as mentioned, this created racial tensions. As employers paid the Blacks lower wages than the white workers, the Blacks tended to be hired first. The white workers, who were also suffering during the famine, resented this labour preference. Lieutenant Governor Parr blamed Nova Scotia's first race riot, in Shelburne, on the inability of the white workers and former soldiers to get their land grants and start supporting themselves and not on the unequal pay and racism on the part of employers. Parr fired the surveyor, Marston, responsible for the preparing the land grants.[132]

Boston King, former slave and one of the community and religious leaders of Birchtown described these hungry years in his journal:

> About this time, the country was visited with a dreadful famine, which not only prevailed at Burch Town but likewise at Chebucto, Annapolis, Digby, and other places. Many of the poor people were compelled to sell their best gowns for five pounds of flour, in order to support life. When they had parted with all their clothes, even to their blankets, several of them fell down dead in the streets, thro' hunger. Some killed and eat their dogs and cats, and poverty and distress prevailed on every side, so that to my great grief I was obliged to leave Burch Town because I could get no employment.[133]

The famine of 1787–1789 eased off and food sources became more readily available. However, this famine would have had terrible consequences for the new settlers, particularly the Black settlers who were treated so harshly. The leaders of Brinley Town knew that something must be done for the community. It was decided that Thomas Peters would go to England and present their petition to the British Government. Peters' trip to England did bring an unexpected alternative to life in Nova Scotia for the Black settlers. It brought the possibility of returning to Africa.[134]

The Evacuation of Most Black Settlements in Nova Scotia

In 1790, after more than five years of waiting for the government to fulfill its promises of land and provisions for the Black Pioneers, Boston King and Joseph Leonard came to believe that the British government had every intention of fulfilling its promises, but that the delivery of these promises was being thwarted at every occasion by the racism and laziness of the provincial government. King organized a petition, outlining their grievances with the way they had been treated. He then travelled, visiting the Black settlements in the Saint John and Annapolis Royal areas. Walker writes: 'Travelling between those two centres he was given power of attorney by 100 Black families in St. (sp) John and another 102 families in Annapolis County, and was authorised by them to go personally to England to deliver the petition'.[135]

But it was Thomas Peters that arrived in England with little more than the petition in his pocket. Through networking in the Black community of London, he was introduced to Granville Sharp and the Sierra Leone Company. Sharp had formed a committee with a group of wealthy philanthropists looking to alleviate the poverty of the Black people of London. According to the Poor Laws of the time, paupers were to be supported by the parish where they were born. As Blacks were considered to have been born in Africa, none of the parishes would take responsibility to help support them.[136] Granville Sharp's committee decided to form a colony for free Blacks in Africa by purchasing land and developing a form of self-governance. The group became known as the Sierra Leone Company. Land was purchased and transport was being organized when Thomas Peters arrived in London. Although he never did get to present at Whitehall, he did join in with the organizers of the Sierra Leone Company and returned to Nova Scotia with news that this company was willing to transport any Black settler who wanted to move to Africa.

A number of books and articles have been written on the exodus of Black settlers in Nova Scotia, including the Jamaican Maroons, to Sierra Leone in 1792 and 1800. Whitfield wrote:

One of the most perplexing gaps in the historiography is the failure to closely observe what happened to the Black community in the

FREE SETTLEMENT

ON THE

COAST OF AFRICA.

THE SIERRA LEONE COMPANY, willing to receive into their Colony such Free Blacks as are able to produce to their Agents, Lieutenant CLARKSON, of His Majesty's Navy, and Mr. LAWRENCE HARTSHORNE, of *Halifax*, or either of them, satisfactory Testimonials of their Characters, (more particularly as to Honesty, Sobriety, and Industry) think it proper to notify, in an explicit manner, upon what Terms they will receive, at SIERRA LEONE, those who bring with them written Certificates of Approbation from either of the said Agents, which Certificates they are hereby respectively authorized to grant or withhold at Discretion.

It is therefore declared by the Company,

THAT every Free Black (upon producing such a Certificate) shall have a Grant of not less than TWENTY ACRES of LAND for himself, TEN for his Wife, and FIVE for every Child, upon such terms and subject to such charges and obligations, (with a view to the general prosperity of the Company,) as shall hereafter be settled by the Company, in respect to the Grants of Lands to be made by them to all Settlers, whether *Black* or *White*.

THAT for all Stores, Provisions, &c. supplied from the Company's Warehouses, the Company shall receive an equitable compensation, according to fixed rules, extending to Blacks and Whites indiscriminately.

THAT the civil, military, personal, and commercial rights and duties of Blacks and Whites, shall be the same, and secured in the same manner.

AND, for the full assurance of personal protection from slavery to all such Black Settlers, the Company have subjoined a Copy of a Clause contained in the Act of Parliament whereby they are incorporated, viz.

———"PROVIDED ALSO, and be it further enacted, that it shall not be lawful
" for the said Company, either directly or indirectly, by itself or themselves, or
" by the agents or servants of the said Company, or otherwise howsoever, to
" deal or traffic in the buying or selling Slaves, or in any manner whatsoever
" have, hold, appropriate, or employ any person or persons in a state of slavery in
" the service of the said Company."

Given under our Hands, LONDON, the 2d Day of AUGUST, 1791.

Henry Thornton, *Chairman*,		Joseph Hardcastle,
Philip Sansom, *Dep. Chairman*,		Thomas Clarkson,
Charles Middleton,		Vickeris Taylor,
William Wilberforce,	Directors.	William Sanford,
Granville Sharp,		Thomas Eldred,
John Kingston,		George Wolff.
Samuel Parker,		

N. B. For the convenience of those who are possessed of property which they cannot dispose of before their departure, the Company will authorize an Agent, who, on receiving from any Proprietor a sufficient power for that purpose, shall sell the same for his benefit, and remit the Purchase-money (through the hands of the Company) to such Proprietor at Sierra Leone.

A call to come to Sierra Leone, posted in Nova Scotia, PANS RG 1 vol. 419 no. 1 (microfilm no. 15460)

Maritimes between 1792 and 1812, except for the experience of the Jamaican maroons. Most studies tend to concentrate on the Black Loyalists who went to Sierra Leone, paying less attention to those who remained behind.[137]

Why did Rose Fortune choose to stay behind in Nova Scotia? The offer of a new life in Africa, where people looked like her, her family and her neighbours, where they would have self-government with no white people treating them as inferior, must have been extremely tempting. There were, however, conditions for going to Sierra Leone. Bridglal Pachai and Henry Bishop, authors of the book *Historic Black Nova Scotia*, write: 'The company's (Sierra Leone) agent, John Clarkson, came to Nova Scotia and New Brunswick to recruit Blacks who qualified to leave (that is, had no debts, were not indentured and were free and willing to go.)'[138] Rose was 18 years old in 1792; Aminta, if she was still alive, would have been in her early 50s. Why did Rose stay behind? Did she have debt at the age of 18? Was her mother ill and not able to go to Sierra Leone, and Rose had to stay behind to nurse her? Did one of them indenture themselves to a white family during the famine and had to keep to the terms of the indenture? Again, as no records have surfaced about Rose's situation during these years (1785–1827), we can only speculate.

The exodus of African-Nova Scotians to Sierra Leone from 1792 to 1800 took almost half of the Black population of Nova Scotia away. What did the Black communities, such as Brinley Town, look like after so many of their members left? Pachai and Bishop write:

The future as they saw it rested in both individual and community initiatives, in using their skills as craftsmen, in tilling their little allotments in isolated and distant place, in building churches and schools for upliftment of dignity, self worth and enlightenment.[139]

CHAPTER 4

Rose on Long Island, Digby Neck

The year was 1793. Brinley Town on the Little Joggin was cold and nearly empty. Where once people desperately needed huts and houses to live in, now many of the huts sat vacant and desolate, with curtains around a window where no one looked out. Whole families, as well as individuals, had left for Sierra Leone. Brinley Town lost more than three quarters of its residents. The remaining people felt abandoned, longing for the company of those who had left, wishing they were headed to the green and warm lands of Africa as well. The roads of Brinley Town were empty of people. Even the dogs and cats looked lost, blinking with wonder at where everyone went. The churches had lost not only most of their enthusiastic Black congregation but also their Black leaders.

Rose was alone, trying not to give in to the tears she felt under her eyelids. She shook her head as if to shake the tears, straightened her shoulders and set her chin at an angle of determination. "I've survived coming here, losing my parents; I've survived the famine, watched some of my friends die. I'll survive this as well."

She walked to the hut of her friend Polly, and together they sat down on the birch bed frame and talked about what to do next. They were both alone with no family, no man and no children.

"Well," Polly said, trying to be optimistic, "at least we can go where we want. We don't have to go where our folks tell us to go or a man tells us to go. We don't have to think about how it will affect our children."

"Yes, but we are alone," Rose said, still trying to stifle her tears. "We have no one who cares about us, who will help us when we are cold and hungry"

Polly reached across to Rose's lap and squeezed her hand. "We've got each other," she said. "And you know that our community, those of us who are left, our brothers and sisters will share what they have."

Rose squeezed Polly's hand back. "Thank you" she whispered.

"And I heard that there is some work in Digby"

"Awww Polly, you know I don't like working in white people's houses, cleaning up after them and them talking down to me," Rose said.

"But that's just it," Polly responded happily. "This work is outdoors. I have been hearing that the fishermen need fish stringers in the worst way. Now that most of our people have gone to Africa, they really need workers and they'll even hire women."

The next day Rose and Polly walked the dusty road into Digby and down to the docks. They asked the fishermen and the women working there if they knew of anyone looking for fish stringers. A man named John Welch hired them on the spot.

"Go back home and get your stuff and meet me here tomorrow morning," he told them. "You'll be needin' to move down the Neck to where I have my fishing grounds and you'll be needin' to keep warm."

Rose and Polly looked at each other. Did they really want to move from Brinley Town?

"It would be a great adventure," Rose said, and she and Polly walked back to Brinley Town, reassuring themselves that this was a good thing. They returned to their huts and packed what little stuff they had. Rose carefully packed her hat and brown coat, wrapped up in a blanket and spent her last night in her hut in Brinley Town. Before the sun rose the next morning, they were on the road, walking back into Digby.

By noon they were on Welch's boat, leaving with the tide that took them from the Annapolis basin and out the Digby Gut. expelling them into the Bay of Fundy. Rose hadn't seen the Bay since she arrived here as a ten-year-old with her parents. That was nearly ten years ago; she was almost 19 now. This memory caused a pang in her heart, but she straightened her back and told herself, "No time for feeling sorry for yourself, Rose. Remember them well and love them well but get on with living."

The boat sailed down the Fundy coast of the Digby Neck and Rose and Polly admired the rugged beauty of the shoreline cliffs and beaches. They stopped briefly at Petit Passage to pick up some more passengers and then continued their trip, coming to Grand Passage, Long Island, with a small island just across the passage at the end of the Neck. The locals called it Brier Island.

For the next two years Rose and Polly worked hard in all sorts of weather

— freezing rain, snow, boiling hot sun. They lived in a hut on the shore with other Black people, where they froze in the winter and baked in the summer. They handled fish — stringing it up, drying it, salting it and packing it up to be put on ships to be taken to other parts of the province or even beyond — to the world. They got around on foot and by rowboat, as water was the main source of transportation at Grand Passage.

Sometimes, when they had time off, they could get transport in a boat that would sail across the Bay of Fundy to the town of Saint John. It was there that Rose met someone.

Joseph lived outside the town of Saint John in another community of Black settlers, just like Brinley Town. Joseph told her how they had also lost a lot of their people, who, deciding that this land of rocks and snow was not the place for them, went on to settle in Africa. He also missed his people and longed to join them on the continent of their ancestors. Joseph and Rose became lovers. Rose took every opportunity she could to go and see Joseph in Saint John. Eventually they found out that she was pregnant.

Joseph professed his love for her but told her he could not leave his job. Rose offered to move to Saint John to be with him. Joseph hung his head low and confessed that he already had a woman in Saint John. They were married. Heartbroken at his betrayal and in a rage with herself for loving him, Rose returned to Grand Passage, and with the help of a midwife had her baby, a girl she named Jane.

Jane was born healthy and in 1795, when the Church of England Reverend Roger Viets travelled down the Digby Neck to perform baptisms and other church duties, he baptized little baby Jane.

"What is your surname?" he asked Rose as he wrote down a record of Jane's baptism in his book.

"I don't have one Reverend," she responded. "My mother and father were slaves and never took on any last name. They sure weren't going to take on their last owner's name."

Reverend Viets was in a conundrum. Most of his Black congregation members had last names, but Rose did not and wouldn't take one. Eventually he recorded, as best he could, the baptism in his book for 1795 in Grand Passage, and then moved on to the next person. Rose was happy. Her child was baptized in the Church of England — her faith and that of her parents.

It was not easy to work and raise a baby by oneself, but Rose got on with the task and she and baby Jane and Polly travelled to other areas where work was available. Sissiboo Falls was another community of free Black folk and Rose and Polly took Jane and lived there for a time. They worked in the forest, leading the horses and oxen out, hauling trees that were felled, taking them to Weymouth to be milled and stacked on the ships.

Baby Jane caught an illness and died at this place. Both Rose and Polly were devastated as Jane had been their baby. Tenderly they wrapped her in a blanket and placed her in a grave, their community minister praying over her tender childish body. For weeks Rose moved about in a haze of grief and despair, barely aware of what she was doing. She only felt better after she decided that, if she ever had another baby girl, she would name her Jane after the baby girl who had died.

After a few years, Rose met another man, hoping that this time she would be offered the love, affection and support she craved so much.

It was not to be. Rose gave birth to a son, John, in Digby and another daughter whom she named Jane, as she had promised herself. With two small children now, Rose continued working and raising her children as best as she could. She worked hard to earn money, hiring friends to look after her children when they were young, leaving them to care for themselves as they got older. The family moved around the area as Rose found work, or love, or both. Sometimes the family lived in the old Clements grant behind Bear

Grand Passage between Long Island and Brier Island, painted by Joseph Frederick Wallet DesBarres in 1780. Was Rose here fifteen years later? Image courtesy of Library of Congress Geography and Map Division.

River, called the Negro Line and sometimes they lived down in Southville, which was also called the Negro Line. They moved around a lot, finding work, love and community. And the three of them got on with living.

Documented Evidence - Rose on Long Island, Digby Neck

This story has been cobbled together with little bits and pieces of evidence that I could find buried deep in museum records, archives or casual mentions in history. It is my belief that Rose worked on Long Island on what is now called Digby Neck, a long piece of land that straddles St. Mary's Bay and the Bay of Fundy.

Reverend Roger Viets recorded in 1795: "A Black female child of Jane a Black woman named Rose."[140] The lack of a simple comma makes this baptism confusing. Is it a Black child named Rose born of a Black woman named Jane, or is it a Black child named Jane born of a woman named Rose? If he had put a comma after the words "a Black woman," we might know who the mother is and who is the child. Or not. Did Viets get their names mixed up calling the mother Jane and the child Rose? I believe he did.

After the exodus to Sierra Leone, there were not many African-Nova Scotian people left in the province. To find a record of two 'coloured' women named Rose and Jane in the same line and in the same geographic vicinity where Rose and her parents landed, is strong evidence that this is Rose Fortune.

Author Reverend Walter Greenwood writes of this baptism in his 1934 book *History of Freeport Nova Scotia 1784-1934* but he adds a comma: "A Black female child of Jane, a Black woman named Rose."[141] The original document does not contain the comma. On page 11, Greenwood writes of this baptism: "There was a negro child baptized at Grand Passage, Long Island, in 1795, of one Rose, a colored woman."[142] That sentence indicates it was a child of Rose that was baptised.

Greenwood mentions a community of Black people at Grand Passage in his 1934 book but does not pay it any particular attention. He remarks that the Loyalist Bartholomew Haines arrived on Long Island with "two servants, that is slaves, with him."[143] Later on, Greenwood writes: "There was a negro burying ground near Ed Walker's house."[144] Grand Passage, Long Island

Government Landing Pier. Freeport. N. S.

Postcard showing Freeport, Digby Neck, Nova Scotia in the 1930s. Photographer unknown. Freeport was known as Grand Passage when Rose was here and had her daughter Jane baptised by Reverend Roger Viets. Today Grand Passage refers to the water between Long Island and Brier Island.

became a busy shipbuilding community, which also had a fishing industry. There would have been jobs for manual labourers, what most Black people were hired to be. The presence of a 'negro graveyard' means that Black people were in Grand Passage in some numbers, living and dying there, but not having their presence recorded by white, Eurocentric historians. How sad. How infuriating.

Aminta disappears from history again

What happened to Aminta? There is no record of her after her arrival in Nova Scotia. Viets was not too meticulous about the accuracy of his burial records of Black people. For example, on November 22, 1790, he recorded the burial of "a Black, woman ... pleurisy."[145] In December 1800 he recorded another burial: "A Black man ... poisoned himself."[146] In June 1803 he recorded "a Black Woman ... of Old Age."[147] Viets did record the burials of several Black people, giving their names if he knew them and what they died of; however, he did not give the same attention to the burials of Black people as he did to those of white people. Was Aminta one of those Black people that were recorded as being buried but her name was not given? If Aminta was the woman buried in 1803, she would have been 69 or 70 years old.

It is interesting to note as well a baptism Viets did in Sissiboo Falls, now known as Weymouth Falls, on June 11, 1797: "Rose Jones, a Black female adult."[148] This could have possibly been Rose Fortune, taking the surname of her male partner, as Jones was a common surname of African-Nova Scotian people in the area at that time. Perhaps Rose was being baptized again to re-affirm her faith.

There was a rumour that Rose gave birth to a daughter that went to Sierra Leone.[149] Local history author Ian Lawrence discounts that rumour, as any daughter of Rose's would have been less than five years old and too young to travel by herself. Unfortunately, the ships lists of the approximately 1200 passengers who went to Sierra Leone have not been found to date.[150]

How old was Jane Fortune?

The census-taking later in the 1800s, which thankfully started listing the names of both men and women, recorded Jane Fortune as being born in approximately 1815 and marrying Isaac Godfrey on December 21, 1830. This would make Jane 15 years old when she married and Isaac around 23. However, if the baptismal record at Grand Passage on Long Island is that of Jane, the daughter of Rose, then Jane was actually 35 years old. She would have been 12 years older than Isaac if Isaac's census records are accurate. Which was Jane's true age? Census takers often made mistakes when recording names and ages. I believe, however, that the Jane Fortune who was recorded as marrying Isaac Godfrey was the second daughter of Rose Fortune, also named Jane.

There was a tradition at this time of naming the next born child after the one who had died. Most genealogists and researchers are aware that census records often have mistakes in them. The census records of Black people would have been even more of a challenge, with a probability of higher numbers of mistakes. Historian Suzanne Morton notes that documents that record the history of Black women are scarce and biased: "African-Nova Scotians were seriously under-enumerated in the census and their entries marked by a high degree of inaccuracy."[151]

Rose takes a Surname

The problem of a lack of surname for Rose must have been becoming an issue. Most of her Black friends had surnames. Some of them took on the last name of their owners, particularly if they felt they had been treated well. Annapolis County has several families of the same surname, but some are white and others are Black. The family name of Ruggles comes from Timothy Ruggles, who attempted to set up his plantation on the North Mountain at Wilmot.[152] Today we come across white people with the last name of Ruggles, descended from Timothy Ruggles and we have Black families with the same surname, descended from some of his former slaves who took on his name.

Other Black settlers wanted nothing to do with the surname of their owners. Perhaps they had been treated badly by their master, they may have been fugitives, or they wanted to shed all vestiges of slavery and chose their own surname. It was probably around the turn of the 19th century that Rose took on her chosen surname or was given a surname — the name of her father, Fortune. She became known, from this point on, as Rose Fortune.

CHAPTER 5

Rose Fortune returns to Annapolis Royal

Rose looked around at the field where she and her father and mother had slept when they first came to Annapolis Royal in 1784. Since she had returned to the town in 1800, many things had changed. There were more buildings and inns for travellers were new, but the streets were all still the same. The wharves had increased in number, with more ship-building and trading going on, and Rose had built up a business for herself around these wharves.

Rose Fortune had come to make a name for herself in the Town of Annapolis Royal when she began finding paid work down at the docks, first helping to move luggage onto the ships, then helping carry travellers' luggage between the ships and the inns. Rose was resourceful though, and when she was not hauling luggage for people, she diversified her business into a Wake Up Service and Boot Polisher.

Eventually Rose saved enough money to purchase an old wooden wheelbarrow to help her move the baggage for her customers. She sometimes piled the luggage of her customers with more concern about efficiency than care, making the townspeople refer to her as a "baggage smasher."

"Move it along," Rose would growl at people who got in the way of her pushing her wheelbarrow piled with heavy luggage. If they did not move fast enough for Rose, she did not hesitate to use her walking stick on them with a short rap on their shoulders to help them move a bit faster.

Rose was sweeping the floor of the St. Luke's Church vestry too vigorously. She had snapped and broken the broom. Muttering mildly under her breath at both herself and the poor quality of the broom, she went to tell the other women who were helping to clean. One of the women wrote down a note that the church needed to purchase a new broom. Rose Fortune was now living in Annapolis Royal and would stay here for the rest of her life. She was 54 years old.

Rose Fortune returned to Annapolis Royal sometime in the early 1800s,

St. Luke's Anglican Church, decorated for Christmas. Photo by Samuel Newton Weare, Annapolis Royal, circa 1930, courtesy of Annapolis Heritage Society.

before 1820. The earliest record of Rose's return was an accident Rose had with a broom. Perkins notes that the accident was recorded in St. Luke's Church account books "1828 — for a whisk broom — the other having been broken by Rose (Fortune)" [153]

Why did Rose became a "baggage smasher"? Charlotte Perkins refers to her in her book, quoting "the late Dr. Robinson," (Dr. Augustus Robinson 1836–1926) who "remembers Judge Haliburton taking the *Maid of the Mist*.......being late it waited for him with old Rose Fortune (coloured), the notorious 'baggage smasher' going ahead"?[154] Suzanne Morton notes that "racism…reinforced class and, unlike their white counterparts, African-Nova Scotian women had virtually no legal wage-earning opportunities outside domestic service, taking in laundry, or sewing."[155] Rose found a way outside domestic service. Family legend among Rose's descendants says that Rose began her baggage handling business at the age of 51, which would have meant that Rose started her business around 1825.[156]

A newspaper article written and published on May 4, 1939 in the *Annapolis Spectator* noted:

> Before 1840…the arrival of the boats from Saint John, with their quota of Halifax-bound Bostonians, was the signal for an old coloured woman named Rose Fortune, then a noted character of the town, to trundle her wheel barrow down to the wharf and carry luggage for the passengers to the stage coach office.[157]

Rural African-Nova Scotian women would have been employed in domestic service of white people's houses. However, they also "spent (time) fashioning split wood baskets or arranging bouquets to be sold at the city market,"[158] which was also an alternative to domestic service. Morton also argues:

Black women were expected to be engaged in hard physical labour such as scrubbing, thereby confirming their unladylike reputation; yet, at the same time, those who restricted their labour to the private domestic sphere and expected their husbands to act as breadwinners could be perceived as lazy.[159]

Baggage handling with a wheelbarrow was certainly hard labour. Rose did not have a husband or man to be a breadwinner for her or her children.

Rose Fortune, "Baggage Smasher", meets Thomas Chandler Haliburton, Lawyer

The early spring breeze was gently swirling dust on the Annapolis Royal street as Rose watched the young man looking over the house. The man looked as though he knew what he was doing, despite his age. He briefly spoke with an older man who gave him some papers to sign. The younger man did so, shook the hand of the older man and then watched him walk away.

The younger man looked in Rose's direction, scanning over her and looking away. He looked back at her again, directly into her face. Rose did not look away but looked back at him. The young man seemed surprised that Rose did not flinch or look away. She was an odd sight, dressed in a man's coat over her dress and wearing a man's wide-brimmed hat. Eventually the young man crossed the street and made his way over to Rose.

"Good morning, my dear," he said to Rose.

"Good morning, sir," she answered back, wondering why he would bother to talk to her.

"My name is Thomas Haliburton," he explained. "I am moving my family and my law practice here from the town of Windsor. My lovely wife Louisa will be looking for a maid and a nanny. Would you be interested in such a position within my household?"

Rose could not help it.......she laughed out loud, a big beautiful burst of laughter showing her white pearls of teeth. "Mister, you are new around here or else you would've never asked me that."

Haliburton was astonished at her laughter from his question. He thought he might be doing her a great favour but here she was, this short-statured, very black woman dressed in men's clothing, laughing at his offer. She obviously didn't know the family he came from. His father was very important and he intended to be as well, starting out in this little mud hole of a town called Annapolis Royal. Haliburton couldn't help it; Rose's laughter made him laugh. The pair of them were standing on the street laughing together and couldn't stop. Tongues in the town clucked as they went by.

"No sir, I won't be your nanny or your maid, but I can find you someone who would be very glad of the job," Rose told him when she caught her breath. "I am my own woman. I find work around the docks and the town, but I will not be a maid nor a nanny to anyone. My name is Rose" she said. "Rose Fortune."

Intrigued, Haliburton looked closer at Rose. She looked to be in her early 40s. "She must have come with the Loyalists," he thought to himself. "I can't imagine this one being a slave. She's too sassy to last long."

"Well then, Rose Fortune, if you would meet me at my inn at 7 tomorrow morning to take my luggage to the docks, I shall pay you, as I have a boat to catch to the town of Digby to see a lawyer there tomorrow," he told her.

They agreed upon this arrangement and at 7 the next morning, Rose was at his inn, trying to get him to move fast enough to catch the boat. Rose cajoled and nudged and pleaded with Haliburton to "Move faster, please, sir," "Move along, please, sir." She wasn't sure how far she could push this white man to move but being polite sure was not getting him to move. She paid a local boy to go and ask the captain of the boat to wait for her while she got this man to the dock and on his way to Digby.

Finally, when Haliburton stepped on to the boat (with a half push from Rose) and just when Rose was thinking she would not ever work for this slow and stubborn man again, he turned around and gave her a big smile. "Thank you, Rose," he said, and gave her a half shilling.

Rose was dumbstruck. A half shilling was a lot of money! She agreed to meet him in the evening when the boat from Digby came back and waved him off.

And so the relationship between Rose Fortune, the business woman and Thomas Chandler Haliburton, the writer and lawyer, began.

Haliburton moved his wife and children to Annapolis Royal a month later, renting the house he had been looking at the day he met Rose. Haliburton's wife was pleasant enough, so were the children and Rose recommended two hard-working women for their house.

Haliburton arranged for Rose to wake him up most mornings, sometimes to catch the boat, the *Maid of the Mist*, to get to Digby, sometimes to get him to go to the local court house within the town. The local townsfolk joked that whenever you saw Haliburton on the street, you were sure to find Rose Fortune just behind him, haranguing him to "Move along, Jedge, move along!"

Rose could talk to Haliburton as no one else was permitted. Some said it was because Rose reminded him of one of his father's slaves, back in Windsor township, who had been like a mother to him; others said it was because Rose and Haliburton were great friends. Regardless of the reason, Haliburton had a bond with Rose and viewed her as someone special.

It was not always easy to get Haliburton moving and Rose often had to hold

Acadian Recorder, July 28, 1821, announcing T.C. Haliburton's office moving to Annapolis Royal.

Thomas Chandler Haliburton, Representative for Annapolis Royal and area, lawyer, judge, author, historian and "friend" to Rose Fortune.

her tongue with him or sometimes use it to boss him around. Haliburton moved with the privileges and entitlement of a white man of status and power. He moved as he wanted, when he wanted, often with threats and cajoling from Rose. He expected people, courts and transportation to wait for him.

Rose turned to look for more business on the wharf but did not see any. She decided to walk up to St. Luke's Church and rest awhile. On her way she passed Father Butler and, looking down at his boots, she muttered to herself, "He looks well and his boots look well." No business there, she decided.

In the early 1830s, Rose and Haliburton said goodbye to each other. Haliburton had received an appointment to a higher court and was leaving with his family to return to Windsor. Rose and her children helped them to pack up their belongings and leave.

Haliburton sent his family on ahead of him via stage coach and, as he and Rose packed up the last of his written stories and legal papers, he turned to her with warmth in his smile. "I shall never forget you, Rose of roses," he told her. He slipped some money to her. "Take care of the children." And he was gone.

Rose, a practical woman, tucked the money into her pocket and turned to the wharves again. "No time to grieve," she told herself. "Just get on with it", and looked for more business to conduct. After all, she had children to support.

Local historian Charlotte Perkins recorded Rose Fortune as being overheard telling Judge Haliburton to "move along, Jedge, move along," as well as her comments to herself on the street while looking at Father Butler's shoes, in her book *The Romance of Old Annapolis Royal*. Judge Haliburton was also overheard calling Rose Fortune "my Black Venus."[160]

Certainly, Haliburton and Rose had an amicable relationship that was noted by other people in Annapolis Royal. She pushed him to do what he was supposed to do and he tolerated her personality, even enjoyed it. It is speculated that the character of Barkin in Haliburton's story *The Old Judge*, was based on Rose Fortune. The name Barkin could be a reference to barking, as in barking orders, which Rose and Barkin often had to do with Haliburton and his character, the Old Judge, to get him to "move along."

Rose Fortune, the Police Officer of Annapolis Royal

"Come along, Jedge, come along" Rose nudged Haliburton one day. Once they finally reached the wharf where the *Maid of the Mist* waited for him, Haliburton turned to Rose with a smile of warmth. "Goodbye, my Black Venus," he said. He slipped a shilling into her hand and tipped his hat to her as he stepped on board the boat bound for the township of Digby.

Rose quickly tucked the shilling into an inside pocket in her coat. She counted on these generous tips to support herself and her children. A couple of young lads were close by; they had noticed the shilling that Haliburton had given her and they circled like hawks after prey.

Rose noticed them moving in closer to her. She pulled her cudgel out of her coat and threatened them with it. "You boys get outta here and don't be bothering me or I'll crack your heads with the end of my stick,"

The lads backed off. They knew that Rose Fortune had strong arms from hauling luggage and they knew that she was not giving them an idle threat. She would use that cudgel if they got too close. Their parents had already warned them to leave her alone lest she beat them. They also knew that if Rose Fortune came upon them in a fist fight amongst themselves or caught them in a brawl with lads from across the river, Rose Fortune would come out the winner.

Late in the evenings, the townspeople of Annapolis Royal could hear Rose Fortune tapping her walking stick, watching out for any problems and making the youth keep the curfew of the town.

Rose Fortune became well known in Annapolis Royal for keeping the peace and order with her walking stick. Running off lads who were trying to impose upon her business probably led to Rose using her stick to keep the peace. As the Annapolis Royal Heritage Society wrote on their website: "Rose became an unofficial policewoman, known for her ability in keeping the more unruly youngsters in order. She was on familiar terms with the leading citizens of town. In other words, she knew everybody." [161]

The descendants of Rose Fortune also knew the legend of their grandmother as the unofficial police officer, having heard the family and town legends passed down from generation to generation.

Rumours of an Underground Railroad

Word had gotten out amongst the slaves in the colonies that the British would let fugitive slaves be free but that, if their masters or slave catchers came looking for them, they would not interfere with their recapture. African people were leaving the south in numbers, running away to Upper Canada. People in Nova Scotia speculated there were runaway slaves coming to this province as well.

There were whispers about an Underground Railroad station for escaped slaves in the village of Clementsport, down the basin, in between the Loyalist town of Digby and Annapolis Royal. It was whispered that a certain ship brought in escaped slaves with each trip down to the thirteen colonies. The crew would sneak them into the village, late at night, using a tunnel that went from a wharf, then underground and up to a dry well up the hill. The ship's captain had to sneak them in, as one of the local families were slave owners that would report any fugitive slaves to their contacts in the States. No one wanted to see slave catchers in the area as they would take any black person, free or not. The rumours were persistent about this tunnel.

Stories abounded in Annapolis Royal about white people seeing fugitive slaves hiding out on the docks at night. It became a local legend that Rose was tapping her stick, not only to warn youth who were out in the town past the curfew, but also to let the hidden and their helpers know when they could come out of hiding. Rose heard the stories about herself and about her conspiracy with runaway slaves and said nothing about it. She would neither confirm nor deny. She let the legend take on a life of its own and kept her stick handy, tapping it rhythmically every now and then just to keep people wondering.

The Peculiar Style of Rose Fortune

Rose was often noted as being peculiar for wearing men's clothing as she worked around the town of Annapolis Royal. Charlotte Perkins wrote, "Her distinctive mode of dressing made her as much an easy mark to locate when needed as the tinkling of a bell of the truck men on the street today."[162] Rose is described by several writers as wearing a man's coat, a man's hat, a short skirt and legged boots.

Rose was also known to smoke a pipe. In the records of the O'Dell House Museum in Annapolis Royal are handwritten notes of a teenage student in 1979. The students were given an assignment to interview elderly people about growing up in the area. The unnamed student decided to interview resident Nellie Lucaw, who was 82 years old. In the student's notes about Nellie Lucaw was a note, "Rose Fortune smoked a pipe."

The wearing apparel of Black women has often been commented upon in negative terms. Author Suzanne Morton notes this in her article" Separate Spheres in a Separate World: African-Nova-Scotian Women in Late 19th Century Halifax County:" "African-Nova Scotian women lived in a bi-cultural world with two distinct historical communities shaping their identities… the culture of the African diaspora and…'the pressure of western culture.'"[163] Morton goes on to write that African-American women were rarely perceived by the dominant culture as "ladies" and that the term lady had "predictable race and class connotations."[164]

Margaret Marshall Saunders was a diarist and author who spent most of her life in Berwick, Nova Scotia, where she was born in 1861. For her writings she was awarded the Order of the British Empire, but, like Haliburton, she wrote racist descriptions of African-Nova Scotian women. Her descriptions of Black women in her journal entries and stories portray African-Nova Scotian women as unrestrained and unladylike, according to her white, middle-class female expectations.[165] Mary Jane Lawson, in her book *The History of the Townships of Dartmouth, Preston and Lawrencetown*, offensively compares the Black women of Preston to monkeys and as "chattering and like them enjoying the warmth and pleasantness of summer."[166]

If African-Nova Scotian women dressed up for special events, such as middle class white women did, they were subjected to mockery. Lawson wrote sarcastically about African-Nova Scotian women "for playing at being real ladies in the festive atmosphere surrounding summer baptisms." Morton went on: "White ladies were protected by the private sphere of motherhood and genteel domesticity, made possible by material circumstances that were not in the resources of most Black women."[167]

Author J.A. Mannette notes the triple burden borne by African-Nova Scotian women: "as members of the subordinate classes, as members of a reviled ethnic group, and as women."[168] In other words, poor, Black and a woman.

The remarks in many publications and passed-down comments about Rose Fortune wearing men's clothing may be attributed to the obvious sexism and racism in reaction to a Black woman having the audacity to wear men's clothing. However, the purpose of her attire is easily explained: Rose was a labourer, pushing a wheelbarrow full of heavy baggage (one could suggest that this would have been mostly the baggage of white men, as they were the ones who could afford to travel and had the freedom to travel unmolested). As a labourer, she needed sturdy and useful clothes such as male labourers wore. Middle-class white women's clothing would simply not do for what Rose was employed in. Though she did adhere to the expected femininity of her gender by wearing skirts, Rose needed the practicality of clothing that allowed her to move, was of a sturdy textile and kept her warm — hence the men's clothing. The man's brown coat and the man's hat would have kept her warm while

The only known image of Rose Fortune, unknown artist; painted circa 1830. Is Rose wearing her father's "Thickset Coat," "a fine Hat, pretty much worn, with a large Brim...a red Flannel Petticoat" that belonged to her mother?

working down at the wharves, where, for two-thirds of the year, the weather is cold and during the winter months, freezing.

There is another simple explanation for Rose's attire: she was wearing her father's coat, her father's hat and her mother's red flannel petticoat. If we re-read the advertisement for Rose's parents as fugitive slaves in 1774, we see an extensive list of clothing they took with them. The famous painting of Rose Fortune shows her wearing clothes similar to the items described in the advertisement: "a Thickset coat…a fine hat, pretty much worn, with a large brim…a red Flannel Petticoat."

Clothing at that time was difficult and expensive to come by.[169] "Their clothing was a local product. At the beginning homespun entirely — Linen, silk and cotton were all too much of a luxury."[170] If Rose was wearing her parents' clothing, the textiles would have been at least 56 years old by the time this painting was done in the 1830s. Textiles were made to be sturdy and durable in those days.[171] It is quite possible that Rose Fortune was wearing the clothes of her parents, who brought these articles with them when they ran away from Virginia.

Rose Fortune as a Mother

Although we know Rose was a single mother, she would have had help with raising her children from her African-Nova Scotian community of friends and family. Whitfield writes that "Black people in the Maritimes created self-sustaining and dynamic communities based on mutual support and shared experience."[172]

Morton notes that the fluidity of the African-Nova Scotian family has remained largely unexamined by historians and sociologists. She writes: "Although no topic in North American history has produced more debate than the discussion of the African-American family, family structure among 19th-century African-Nova Scotians is unexplored."[173] She warns white Eurocentric readers and writers of African-Canadian history: "This fluid household structure cautions us against imposing a preconceived definition of the private family."[174]

Mannette notes: "The fact that marriages performed by Black ministers were illegal had led Walker to refer to Black marital relations as 'casual.'"[175] In other words, all marriages that Joseph Leonard may have performed in Brinley

Town would be considered not legally binding by the white, British-dominated Church of England.

The birth order and dates of Rose Fortune's three children are the subject of much speculation. Genealogists realize that often birth dates are estimated based on ages of other children, birth rates, ages of mothers and other such demographics. The records of birth and death for many people were often not accurately recorded. As a result, we have no definitive records of the birth dates and order of Rose Fortune's three (known) children.

Rose may have very well been married or living with a man when she had any of her children. The fact of her relationships may not have been recorded in the Church or government records of her day. That Rose took her father's name as her surname and gave the surname of Fortune to her children as well suggests that her relationship(s) with their father(s) did not last or were not formalized. Today we would refer to these marital breakdowns as separation and divorce. Rose shared her surname of Fortune with her children and they accepted this name as their own.

Mannette also notes that the Black family did not have the same structure as a white, middle-class British family. Instead, the Black family was an extended kin network that embraced "many who could claim no blood or marriage ties."[177] She notes that English abolitionist John Clarkson was surprised by the strength and ties of the fluid African-Nova Scotian families:

John Clarkson also noticed the strength of family ties among the Black Loyalists and pointed out that the "family" went beyond the normal British definition to include Godchildren or simply people from the same community. He found it curious that Black parents would bring up children of others as if they were their own, without distinction between natural children and ones thus "adopted."[178]

Walker adds that this custom, which was widely observed in Black American slave society, has been traced to West African pre-slave origins. In any case, it seems entirely likely that many aspects of the familial relationship were well established before the migration to Nova Scotia.[179]

The Court Cases of Rose Fortune

It was a sunny morning on June 4, 1839. Rose sat and looked at the scribblings on the paper that had just been delivered to her. She knew it was not good news; things in writing rarely were to her. Rose was missing the company of Haliburton right now. He would have read this for her and then taken care of it. As Haliburton had left years ago, Rose did not have a strong ally any more.

Rose took the paper to a friend of hers who read it and told her that she was being charged, again, with Keeping a Disorderly House. Rose snorted in derision. She had been charged with the same True Bill in 1836 and found Not Guilty. Someone was obviously upset with her keeping the peace in town and was making complaints against her, trying to get her to leave the town.

"I am not even gonna bother showing up" she announced. "Maybe they'll even forget about it. I was found not guilty last time. Why are they trying this again?"

But the courts did not forget and a bench warrant was issued for Rose Fortune's arrest. Rose was brought to court and told that she had to show up to answer the True Bill against her for Keeping a Disorderly House.[180]

The Disorderly Houses Act of 1751 was an Act of the Parliament of Great Britain in force in the 1830s in the British colony of Nova Scotia. Section 8 of the Act, which would have been applied to Rose, read:

> And whereas, by reason of the many subtle and crafty contrivances of persons keeping bawdy-houses, or other disorderly houses, it is difficult to prove who is the real owner or keeper thereof, by which means many notorious offenders have escaped punishment, any person who shall at any time hereafter appear, act, or behave him or herself as master or mistress, or as the person having the care, government, or management of any bawdy-house or other disorderly house, shall be deemed and taken to be the keeper thereof, and shall be liable to be prosecuted and punished as such, notwithstanding he or she shall not in fact be the real owner or keeper thereof.[181]

Did Rose keep a bawdy house or a brothel? Or was she being charged with a law that was not written down but was applied to African-Nova Scotians?

The Grand Jury filed a True Bill against Rose Fortune for Keeping a Disorderly House. NSARM, RG-34-301 Vol. 1 Grand Jury Book 1801-1861, April Sessions 1839.

Annapolis ss. ... General Sessions of the Peace April Term
The King
vs
Isaac Roach and Jeremiah V. Buskirk

Isaac Roach and Jeremiah V. Buskirk appeared under their Recognizance to receive the Judgment of the Court. Sentenced Isaac Roach to pay a fine to Our Sovereign Lord the King of Two Shillings and Sixpence and Jeremiah V. Buskirk a fine of One Pound Ten Shillings and costs of prosecution taxed at Five Pounds Five Shillings and Sixpence.   S. Cowling Clk.

The King
vs   Indictment for Keeping a disorderly house
Rose Fortune

Indictment traversed. Rose Fortune arraigned pleaded Not Guilty, Jury impanelled & sworn Witnesses sworn and examined Jury charged, retire and return a Verdict of Not Guilty. The said Rose Fortune discharged by Proclamation
                    S. Cowling Clk.

The King
vs
Charles P. Bailey, John Wade the third and James LeSueur
Indictment for a riot and assault.
John Wade the third arraigned under this Indictment pleaded Not Guilty entered into recognizance to appear at November Term next. Charles P. Bailey entered into recognizance to appear at November Term next. James L. Sueden called answered not.   S. Cowling Clk.

The King
vs   Recognizance to appear
Samuel Videto, William LeCain &   The said Samuel Videto
William Ritchie   called answered not
Recognizance estreated,

                    Saml Cowling Clk.

In the middle of the page, The King vs. Rose Fortune in the Indictment for Keeping a disorderly house...Jury charged, notice and return a Verdict of Not Guilty. NSARM RG 34-301 (P) Records of the Court of Quarter Sessions 1839-1929

Walker writes about rules for the Black settlers in 1799:

In Shelburne hand bills were published by the magistrates "forbidding Negro Dances, and Negro Frolicks in this Town." When this by-law was contravened the offending Blacks were charged with "Riotous Behaviour" and sent to the House of Correction. A second offence might mean being "ordered out of their homes for keeping a disorderly house."[182]

Were these rules also being applied in other African-Nova Scotian communities across Nova Scotia in 1835? As Rose was charged with keeping a disorderly house twice within five years, it seems as if someone did not want Rose living in her house in town and was trying to force her to move.

Archival records of 1836 show in the Annapolis Supreme Court "In the Indictment the King vs. Rose Fortune for Keeping a Disorderly House."[183] By 1839, King William IV had died, and Queen Victoria had assumed the throne. On June 4, 1839, records show up as "The Queen vs. Rose Fortune Indictment for Keeping a Disorderly House. Rose Fortune was called, answered not. Bench warrant issued." In September 1839 "Rose Fortune called under Bench Warrant and entered into recognizance to appear at April Term 1840."[184]

Unfortunately, there are no transcripts of the trials of Rose Fortune, although records show that in 1836, Rose was charged and found not guilty.[185] We do not know the outcome of the trial in 1840 as the court records for the Court of Annapolis April Term 1840 have been lost.

Rose in Receipt of Money

Rose was in a hurry. Word had gotten around the town of Annapolis Royal that Alfred Whitfield, the provincial representative for the area, was giving out money to be distributed amongst the coloured people of Annapolis and Birch Town outside Lequille. She knew that William Ruggles and Henry Moses had received some money; Widow Halliday had received less than them, but still, money was money.

Although Rose Fortune no longer had to support her children as the year was 1851 and her children were grown, Rose was growing physically tired of the work she was doing. A bit of money would certainly be welcome.

Rose arrived at Whitfield's office and received two pennies. Her name was recorded along with other names and the document was filed away.

"Account of the Expenditures of (5 shillings?) distributed by Messrs Geo Runciman & Thos (Easson?) among the Colored People of Burch Town Settlement and Annapolis last year /51 sent by Alfred Whitfield Esq M.P.P."[186]

Annapolis County had a settlement called Burch/ Birch Town at this time. It was a small settlement of Black people located on what we now know as the Clementsvale Road, outside the town of Annapolis Royal. There were several settlements of Black people named Birchtown that were scattered throughout Nova Scotia. All of them were named after General Samuel Birch, who signed the majority of Certificates of Freedom for the fugitive slaves. The A.F. Church Map of 1876 shows an E. Godfrey living in that location.[187] The Birchtown settlement of Annapolis County was located in what is now known as Princedale, close to the turnoff leading to Milford and the Number 8 highway.[188]

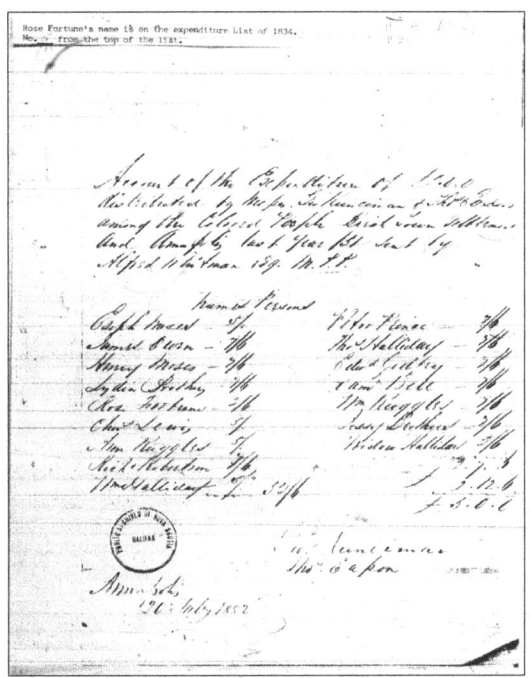

An account document showing that Rose Fortune received money from Alfred Whitfield, Esq. Rose is the fifth name down, left column showing how much she received. Nova Scotia Archives, mfm 15108, vol. 19, #48

Rose Fortune, along with several others, received part of the five shillings as members of the local African-Nova Scotian community. Rose would have been 76 or 77 years old at this time.

Rose Fortune meets Colonel Sleigh

The next year, 1852, Rose was 78 years old and particularly feeling her age. She was living in town with her granddaughter, Amberzine Lewis. Their house was located close to the wharves and Amberzine's husband Albert worked on the wharves and often helped Rose with her business.

Rose started awake from dozing. She was late! Rose knew that the Belchers Line stage coach from Halifax must have arrived by now and she might be missing some business. She hoisted herself from her comfortable chair and put her old hat and coat on. Firmly grabbing the handles of her wheelbarrow, she moved in the mist of the June evening, down the street toward the wharves where the stage coach had come in and dispatched its travellers.

It was this same evening that a tired Lieutenant Colonel Sleigh, as he fancied calling himself, arrived in Annapolis Royal from Halifax on the stage coach. He had recently spent some uncomfortable time in a jail in Charlottetown, Prince Edward Island, were he had been charged and convicted of fraud. After he was released from jail, Sleigh made his way to Halifax, where he caught the stage coach to Annapolis Royal. Sleigh was on his way to Saint John, New Brunswick and would catch the ship in the morning. Meanwhile, he needed an inn for the night.

He moved toward the inn that the stage coach driver had recommended to him. Shown to his room by the innkeeper, Sleigh noticed that his room was not particularly commodious, but he was willing to shrug it off as he was tired and hungry.

"Innkeeper, I am hungry and fatigued and need some victuals," he demanded.

"None to be got," the innkeeper responded. "It was market day today. All is eaten. Most I can give you is fried pork and tea."

Sleigh, not one to accept less than he thought was his due, immediately demanded that his luggage be packed back up and taken out into the street. He would not stay at this inn that night with that abominable innkeeper, he told himself.

The innkeeper obliged Sleigh's demands, only too happy to throw this snob and his luggage back out into the street.

Sleigh stood there in the dirt as the mist swirled around him and the evening light was falling, wondering what to do next. As he stood there pondering, he saw a most curious sight coming down the street toward him.

An old, short Black woman dressed in men's clothing and pushing a wheelbarrow came down the street toward him. People on the street who saw her coming jumped out of her way. Those who did not see her coming felt the end of her stick on their backs as she growled at them to move along.

"Do you need yer luggage moved, sir?" the old woman asked him.

"Indeed, I do," Sleigh answered. "I want a better inn than this one. Do you know of one that is available?"

I do, sir," she answered. "Much better than this fleabag place and more fittin' for a gentleman such as yerself."

The old woman hoisted his luggage up and threw it in her wheelbarrow. Sleigh cringed slightly at the thought of his beautiful leather bag being scuffed in her primitive wooden wheelbarrow, but he was more curious than upset.

He followed the old woman up the street to another larger inn where he dined well with slices of beef, a pudding and a glass of port. Later that evening, he wrote in his journal about his encounter with this curious old woman.

> During the bustle attendant upon this rapid proceeding, I was aided in my hasty efforts to quit the abominable Inn, by a curious old Negro woman, rather stunted in growth, as black as the ace of spades and dressed in a man's coat and felt hat, she had a stick in her hand which she applied lustily to the backs of all who did not jump instantly out of the way. Poor old dame. She was evidently a privileged character.[189]

Sleigh had been a lieutenant in 1844 in the 77th Regiment of Foot, meaning he oversaw a battalion. A lieutenant colonel, which Sleigh was not, oversaw a regiment. Sleigh sold his commission as a lieutenant in 1848, when he was 27 years old, and involved himself in various ventures. By 1852 he found himself in

Lieutenant-Colonel B.W.A. Sleigh, as he fancied calling himself. Sleigh met and conversed with Rose Fortune, recording this interaction in his journal. Photographer unknown, date unknown, courtesy of Sailstrait blog site.

Lower Saint George Street, by the ferry and the wharves, Annapolis Royal, 1851. Rose Fortune met Lieutenant Colonel Sleigh on this street seven years later. He recorded their meeting in his journal. Photo courtesy of Annapolis Royal Heritage Society.

Charlottetown, opening his own bank — the Bank of Charlottetown, in which "Captain Sleigh is President." Many accolades and honours ensued.

Two months later it was over. The assets of the "bank" were seized and Sleigh found himself in jail for selling the rights to an estate to which he did not have title.

Sleigh was out of jail by the end of the year, began calling himself "Lieutenant Colonel" and resumed his travels once again.[190]

Without a doubt, Sleigh was describing Rose Fortune. Rose was 78 years old and still working as a baggage handler. Rose was also still handling loiterers and wayward lads with a stick in her hand.

The reference Sleigh made to Rose as "a privileged character" has stuck to the legend of Rose Fortune. In later years the label was used with good intentions; however, it is ironic that a white man, fresh out of jail, with enough money to travel and stay at the more luxurious inns, would call an economically poor old Black woman, still working at a hard labour job a "privileged character." Did he mean that people of the town tolerated her behaviour? Sleigh did not realize that Rose Fortune was considered the unofficial police officer in Annapolis Royal. The town was privileged to have Rose Fortune keep the sailors, soldiers and young lads in line as an unpaid police officer.

The Death of Rose Fortune

Rose was lying in bed close to the wood stove in Amberzine's house. She barely had the energy to get up any more. At the age of 90, Rose congratulated herself for living so long and gave herself permission to keep lying in bed and enjoying the heat of the wood stove on this cold February 20th day in 1864.

Rose was rambling over memories in her mind. "It is true," she thought to herself. "The older you get, the sharper your oldest memories become."

Rose thought a great deal about her parents. In her old age, she was missing them. Her children, the ones who had survived childhood, had been living their own lives for many years now with their own problems and joys. They had children of their own, some of whom had survived, while some had not. Rose even had a great-granddaughter who was named after her, as her grandchildren regarded their grandmother so highly. Amberzine and Albert and their children agreed to take care of Rose in her advanced years.

Amberzine was born in 1844, when Rose was 70 years old. Amberzine married Albert Lewis of Lequille and they had 12 children together, with one daughter being called Rosanna — shortened to Rosie-Francis.[191] Albert Lewis took over Rose's baggage handling business and it became known as Lewis Transfer.[192]

James Lewis, son of Albert and Amberzine Lewis, carrying on the family business, started by his great grandmother Rose Fortune. James Lewis was the father of Daurene Lewis, the first African-Canadian female mayor in Canada. Photo courtesy of Parks Canada.

The gravestones of Rose Fortune's daughter, Jane Godfrey (on the right) and son in law, Isaac Godfrey (on the left). It is believed that Rose is buried near Jane in an unmarked grave. Photo courtesy of Denise Rice.

Rose sighed with comfort and rolled over on her side. As she did so, she saw her father for the briefest instant. He was young and healthy and smiling at her. It felt good to see him. Her mother had been making herself known to her in the past few days as well, standing outside the bedroom window and looking in on her as if to say, "Are you ready yet? Come with me!"

Rose knew that they were beckoning her to join them. Her time to be with them again was coming. It was none too soon, Rose thought to herself. She was tired of this place, her time on earth. She had done her best with her long life despite all the obstacles that were thrown in her path. She was satisfied with what she had done, the children she had raised, the businesses she had created and the problems she had overcome.

She closed her eyes and pulled the quilt up closer to her, snuggling into her downy white pillow. Rose Fortune smiled as she fell asleep one last time.

Rose Fortune died February 20, 1864 and is believed to be buried in an unmarked grave where, eventually, her daughter Jane and son-in-law Isaac Godfrey were buried. This would be in the "Black Section" in the Old Military Graveyard in Annapolis Royal.

Perkins wrote about this in her book about the Romance of Old Annapolis
Royal:

> Quite a number of the Negro population of the days gone by of this
> vicinity are buried in the old military cemetery in this town. The south-
> east corner of the cemetery seems to have been allotted especially to
> them. There they lie under the shadow of the old willows, their graves
> for the most part unmarked by any stone to identify their last resting
> place.[193]

Rose was a 'character' in Annapolis Royal and elsewhere. She was born in
a time when, as a poor Black woman, she was expected to keep her place in
the community and keep herself silent. She did neither. Rose ran up against
difficulties time after time and overcame them, time after time. She managed
to survive grueling times, she dealt with racism daily, she dealt with misogyny
daily and she dealt with poverty daily. She raised her children, she owned and

St. George Street, Annapolis Royal, looking down toward Land's End, with
the Annapolis Basin to the left. Rose Fortune lived in a house on this street to
the right of this photo, near the site of the present Royal Bank of Canada, on
the corner of Victoria Street and St. George Street. This photo was taken by
an unidentified photographer in 1860, four years before Rose Fortune died.
Courtesy of Annapolis Heritage Society.

ran several small businesses and she was considered the town's police constable. She earned the respect of the townspeople of Annapolis Royal and area and left a substantial legacy.

In doing so, Rose Fortune, in her own way, did early work toward eradicating racism, misogyny and poverty. We still have a long way to go, even as this book is being written nearly 250 years later, but Rose helped push this along. An amazing woman of grit and resilience, Rose would take none of the grief that was imposed upon her and instead carried on with her life as best as she could. We, the people who have gotten to know Rose Fortune, are the privileged characters.

The Legacy of Rose Fortune

"The story of Rose Fortune was just part of growing up and being a Lewis in Annapolis Royal."

— Daurene Lewis, descendant, 1989[194]

Rose Fortune has thousands of descendants all over the world. Some of her descendants stayed in the Annapolis Royal area, but many moved to urban areas such as Halifax, while others moved to Toronto. Almost all of them moved for better job opportunities; many say they moved because of small town racism.

> "At the time I was growing up in Annapolis Royal, the dances were segregated and segregation was very evident in the area," said Daurene Lewis, descendant of Rose Fortune, in an interview in 1989.[199] Lewis and her mother and grandmother all lived in the town of Annapolis Royal, with Daurene eventually becoming the mayor. She was the first African-Canadian female mayor in Canada. Lewis earned many accolades: 'The Order of Canada; the United Nations Global Citizenship Award; the Progress Club of Halifax Woman of Excellence Award for Public Affairs and Communication; and the Nova Scotia Black Cultural Centre's 'Wall of Honour'.[195]

Many of Rose's descendants have gone on to fight against racism and achieve goals, both personal and community-based. One of Rose's grand-

Bust of Daurene Lewis by Ruth Abernathy, in Lewis Plaza, Annapolis Royal, September 2018, photo by author.

daughters married into the family of Aesop Moses, descendant of one of the two slaves of the Davoue family of Annapolis Royal that arrived in Annapolis Royal at the same time as Rose Fortune and her parents. Some of Rose's descendants moved to Boston for job prospects, establishing a home base at 18 and 22 Wheeler Street, where several family members lived while working

The *Fundy Rose* marine vehicle ferry, named after Rose Fortune in 2015. The ferry runs between Digby, Nova Scotia, and Saint John, New Brunswick, two places where Rose spent time. Photo courtesy of Bay Ferries.

Descendants of Rose Fortune gather and sit on the memorial to Rose in the Old Garrison Graveyard on the grounds of Fort Anne, Annapolis Royal. It is believed that Rose is buried here in an unmarked grave next to her daughter Jane Godfrey and son in law Isaac Godfrey. Photo courtesy of the *Spectator*.

in Boston. Rose's descendants are scattered all over the city of Boston, working at various careers and avocations.[196]

The Lewis Transport Company, which operated into the 1960s, was run by descendants of Rose Fortune, who took over her baggage transfer business when Rose became too old and ill to run it anymore. Others were workers on the docks, on ships and on trains – as sailors, teamsters and porters. Descendants married into families from Barbados, the West Indies and Africa.[197] They have been taught about the legend of their ancestor Rose Fortune and revere the memory of her.

"I will tell you that Emma's middle name is Rose," Peter Nkansah, descendant of Rose Fortune and nephew of Daurene Lewis said, his voice choked with emotion. "That was a promise that I made at Daurene's service back in Halifax a number of years ago. We knew that we were pregnant at the time

Poster for the play *Fortune*, written by George Cameron Grant and performed in New York in 2014.

and I said, "Well, the roots running as deep as they are, and all the kindnesses that have been shown, we're going to keep it going."[198]

Rose Fortune's memory has been revered and honoured in other ways. The Association of Black Law Enforcers offers an annual scholarship called the Peter Butler III — Rose Fortune Scholarship.[199] In 2018 Rose Fortune, nominated by Alan and Durline Melanson on behalf of The Historical Association of Annapolis Royal, was designated a person of national historic significance who helped to define Canada's history.[200] Annapolis Royal has named its main plaza the Lewis Plaza, after Rose and her descendant Daurene, where there is now a bust of Daurene Lewis on display.[201]

The ferry that runs between Digby and Saint John, N.B. was named the Fundy Rose, in honour of Rose Fortune. It was nominated by the village of Inglewood outside of Bridgetown, in 2015.[202]

On Canada Day, July 1, 2017, a monument to Rose Fortune was unveiled in the old Garrison Graveyard, on the grounds of Fort Anne. The monument is Fortune's wheelbarrow, wharf and headstone, made into a bench.[203]

After being introduced to the story of Rose Fortune by heritage interpreter Alan Melanson during The Historical Association of Annapolis Royal's Candlelight Graveyard Tour, George Cameron Grant, a New York playwright, wrote a play about Rose Fortune that has been performed several times.

Documentary films have been made about Rose Fortune, many of them imagining what Rose's early life was like. Unfortunately, historical evidence was not available to write her complete story. Even now, the fragments of historical research found for this book only tell a partial story. More evidence may come to light over the coming years to give us a clearer picture of Rose's life in Nova Scotia. Let us hope that it does. And let us continue to celebrate this remarkable woman — Rose Fortune.

Appendix 1: Brinley Town

There is no written evidence that currently names Rose Fortune as a citizen of Brinley Town in what was then Annapolis County. However, pieces of research findings have lead me to believe that Rose was there and in the area for many of the years after she arrived in Annapolis Royal. I theorize this for several reasons:

First is the geography: Brinley Town, outside of the new town of Digby, was easily accessible from Annapolis Royal by water. Rose and her mother would not have to move too far or take a long trip across water, through the forest or a combination of both.

Second, Brinley Town was the second largest community of Free Blacks in Nova Scotia, with the first being Birchtown, outside of Shelburne. Brinley Town had plans for their own churches and schools when they settled the community with the Black Pioneers. To have her own church and an education for her child must have sounded wonderful to Rose's mother, Aminta, who was now on her own with her 10-year-old daughter in another country.

Third, although the town of Digby still had slave owners, they did not have them to the extent that Annapolis Royal did. Annapolis Royal and area had the slave-owning families of DeLancy, Ditmar, Totten, Davoue, Sinclair, Croscup, O'Dell, Hatfield, Barclay, Ruggles and Bonnett, to name a few. In addition, Annapolis Royal was overcrowded with Loyalists and there was very little room for anyone, rich or poor. Leaving to go with a community of more than 200 free Blacks, away from the slave-owners in the town of Annapolis Royal, away from the chance of re-enslavement, would make sense to one as vulnerable as a single Black woman and her child.

Fourth, all three of Rose's children married the children of a Brinley Town family. Jane married Isaac Godfrey, son of Edward Godfrey and wife Unknown, of Brinley Town. John married Hester Godfrey, sister to Isaac and son of Edward Godfrey and wife Unknown. Margaret married John Francis, son of Charles Francis and wife Unknown of Brinley Town.

Fifth, the Black communities of Granville Ferry, Inglewood, Delaps Cove and Thorne's Cove were not yet settled or even conceived. Granville Ferry had a settlement of Blacks by the 1820s but that was still long after Rose and Aminta's time of the 1780s.

The Black community located in Thorne's Cove, Karsdale, started in

1785, the year after Brinley Town was established, when free Black Edward Jackson purchased 100 acres of shore and land for five shillings.[204] They eventually built a road over the mountain to connect themselves with family and neighbours who lived in the Black community of Delaps Cove, which was established by 1806.[205] Delaps Cove had a church and school and many of the residents intermingled with and had children with the Mi'kmaq, being as isolated as they were in the forests of Annapolis County. The community came to refer to this mix of races as Black Indians.[206] This community was still vibrant up until the 1950s when the school was closed down and the children were bused to other schools. The last house of the settlement, belonging to fisherman Charles Marsman, burned down after 2013.[207] Foundations still exist at the former settlement, which has been the target of vandals in recent years.[208]

The history of Inglewood is not readily recorded to my knowledge. Local historian Elizabeth Coward-Ruggles writes briefly in her book *Bridgetown Nova Scotia: Its History to 1900 about Inglewood*: 'Many of these names in the census of 1860 belong to coloured people either living in Inglewood or in the town, so this seems a good place to write about that little settlement, now nearly a hundred years old'.[209] It is assumed that Coward-Ruggles is referring to the time she is writing the book, the early 1950s, and not the census of 1860.

The website of Map Annapolis has a series of maps in which they locate the settlements and homes of historic Black communities. This website records Inglewood as being settled by Black people in 1850.[210]

Sixth, Brinley Town has a large population of Church of England followers. Rose was a follower of the Church of England. Birchtown, outside of Shelburne, although it was also Church of England, was as far away as was Preston, outside of Halifax, which was mainly Baptist. The Black community outside of Liverpool was mainly Methodist. As religion was very important in the day-to-day life of people of all races in Nova Scotia during this time period (1780–1800), Rose would want to be with other members of her congregation and her religion. As Brinley Town was mainly Church of England, it would make sense that Rose and her mother would go with them.

Did Rose move from Brinley Town to Grand Passage on the Digby Neck (now known as Freeport) and give birth to Jane and subsequently have her baptised? The baptismal record of Reverend Roger Viets suggests that Rose did just that. The lack of a surname of both Rose and Jane suggests that these two females were descendants of a fugitive slave who was not given nor took a surname.

Finally, we examine the seventh piece of evidence that Rose was in Brinley Town. After the Black exodus to Sierra Leone in 1792, I believe Rose left the community to go to work on Long Island, Digby Neck. Jane Godfrey's last will and testament (written December 19, 1885), read after her death on January 10, 1886, gives us further evidence of Rose and her children in and around Brinley Town and area. Jane Godfrey leaves assets of 'One Trunk of Clothes, My Winter Sacque (sic), The Clock, One Tablecloth, also the residue of any money after all expenses are paid' to '*Priscilla Hatfield of Digby Neck, my particular and Kind Friend*'.[211] (emphasis mine).

Through this research and reasoning, I came to conclude that Rose and her mother were in Brinley Town and the nearby area for much of the missing years of 1785 to 1828. My conclusions may be wrong, but until evidence comes to light that corrects my hypothesis, I envision Rose Fortune on the shores of the Annapolis Basin after she and her parents left New York in 1783. I see Rose Fortune here, in Annapolis Royal, for the rest of her life.

Appendix 2: The DNA tests

When thinking about writing a book about a historical character whose life has not been well documented, a writer has to brainstorm about every option available to help them find the evidence of that person. In considering Rose Fortune, the idea of a DNA test came to mind.

When driving to our home in Perotte, I pass through the village of Lequille, where many of Rose Fortune's local descendants live. In the 23 years that I have lived in the area, I have made friends with several of the residents of this area who are Rose's descendants. If I didn't know them, my husband Kent did, as he went to school with them. As teenagers in the same school, they often socialized together.

When I first met Maggie O'Donnell and her sister Ina Cromwell in Kentville to talk about writing this book, they were a bit apprehensive. Later in the conversation, I mentioned that I was married to Kent Folks. All apprehension evaporated. They had great stories to tell me about hanging out with Kent.

Maggie enthusiastically agreed to do a DNA test. Two other residents of Lequille, James Stevenson and his wife Linda (Currie) Stevenson, both descendants of Rose Fortune, also agreed to do DNA tests. We decided to go with Ancestry.ca DNA tests. While we were waiting for the results of these tests, I found the runaway slave ads of Fortune and Aminta. If this was the Fortune I was looking for, the DNA tests should back this up.

Then I also came across the website of Radiant Roots, Boricua Branches http://radiantrootsboricuabranches.com/ which traces the descendants of Malagasy slaves. There, in the middle of some very long and complicated explanations of reading DNA test results, was a paragraph about Rose Fortune and her parents.[212] Sure enough, the first DNA test results came in and there it was … the tests revealed that Fortune had likely descended from people in Madagascar and Aminta had Andean ancestry. Teresa Vega, in her blog on Malagasy Roots, writes that most Ancestry.ca DNA tests have Malagasy descendants showing up having a large part of Cameroon/Congo components of DNA along with Asian components. This, she says, makes sense, as Madagascar did trade with Asian countries such as Polynesia, Vietnam and the Philippines.[213]

These are the results of the DNA tests of Rose Fortune's descendants:

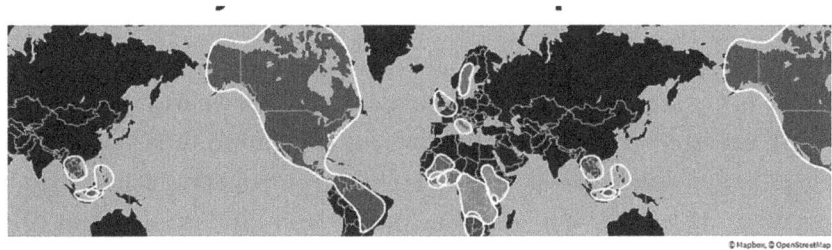

© Mapbox, © OpenStreetMap

Ethnicity Estimate

Cameroon, Congo, and Southern Bantu Peoples	40%	Southeast Asia—Vietnam	1%
Benin/Togo	29%	Italy	1%
Ivory Coast/Ghana	15%	Eastern Africa	1%
Mali	5%	Sweden	1%
Africa South-Central Hunter-Gatherers	2%		
England, Wales & Northwestern Europe	2%	**Migrations**	
Philippines	2%	North Carolina African Americans	
Native American—North, Central, South	1%		

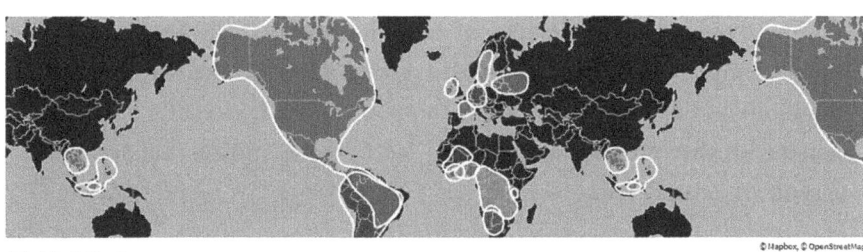

© Mapbox, © OpenStreetMap

Ethnicity Estimate

Cameroon, Congo, and Southern Bantu Peoples	41%	Africa South-Central Hunter-Gatherers	1%
Benin/Togo	31%	Native American—Andean	1%
Ireland and Scotland	9%	Native American—North, Central, South	1%
Ivory Coast/Ghana	6%	Sweden	1%
Germanic Europe	2%	Southeast Asia—Vietnam	1%
Philippines	2%	France	1%
Mali	2%	Baltic States	1%

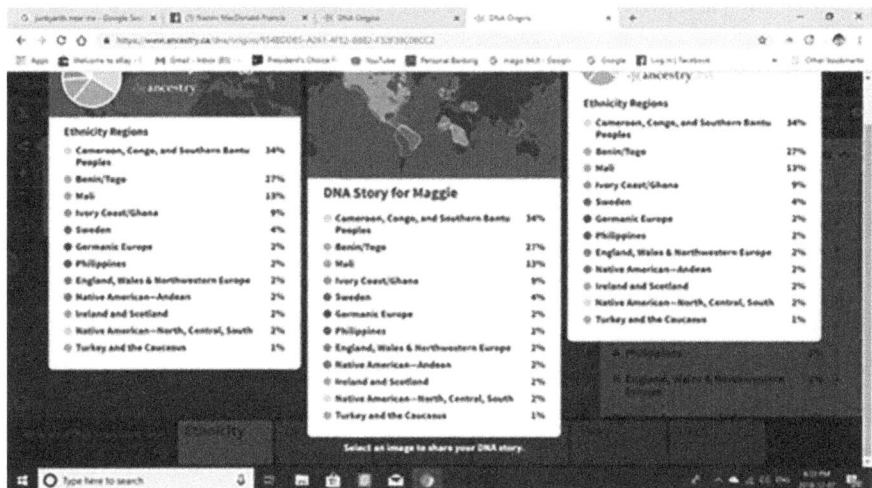

Even though the country of Madagascar is not shown as being included in the visuals, if you go into the DNA detail, it shows up. As Vega points out, the people of Cameroon and Bantu had often migrated from Madagascar.

On Ancestry DNA, we definitely see a combination of East/South/Central Africa geographical areas along with an Asian component which isn't surprising since Madagascar was settled by people from SE Asia and East Africa. Regarding the African geographical areas, one of the things Fonte noted is that, in addition to SE Bantu as a region, one also sees that the Cameroon/Congo region is also somewhat high. The Cameroon/Congo admixture may be coming from Mozambique. This no doubt reflects how the Bantu Expansion spread from West to East Africa.[214]

The Cameroon/Congo region shows up in the DNA tests as 40%, 41% and 34% along with a small Southeast Asian ethnicity. The South Amerindian shows up as well in all three DNA tests. I believe the results of these DNA tests prove that the runaway slave ad for Fortune and Aminta are about the parents of Rose Fortune.

According to Vega, slaves from Madagascar were worth more than slaves from West Africa but she does not explain why. Slave trading from Madagascar went on until the 1790s. It ended only because it became more expensive and hazardous, because of piracy in the Indian Ocean, to ship Malagasy slaves than to ship African slaves. Rose Fortune has ancestry in Madagascar and in South America, proven by the DNA test results.

Appendix 3: Thomas Chandler Haliburton, "No Friend to Abolition"

Haliburton may have had a friendly relationship with Rose Fortune, but he was not a believer in equal rights or equal relationships with African-Nova Scotians. Many of his writings, although culturally acceptable at the time, are now considered overtly racist and sexist. African-Nova Scotian poet and author George Elliott Clarke wrote: "He was no friend of abolition."[215] Clarke, who has examined the writings of Haliburton in relation to African-Nova Scotians, argues that Haliburton wanted a return to "Tory-ism of the Loyalist class." He writes: "Haliburton shared the paternalistic slave-holder's belief that merit — interpreted as white skin, maleness, European ancestry and social rank — determined one's special freedoms, privileges, rights and responsibilities.... The mixing of classes and races was, Haliburton implies, a recipe for social catastrophe."[216]

One of several controversial portrayals of African-Nova Scotians in Thomas Chandler Haliburton's writings Sam Slick. Sketch by Charles William Jeffries (Ryerson Press, 1956).

In his short story *The White Nigger*, about the annual auctioning of poor white people and published in 1836, Haliburton's character Sam Slick states that he and his fellow Americans "deal only in niggers — and those thick skulled, crooked shanked, flat footed, long heeled, wooly headed gentlemen, don't seem fit for much else but slavery."[217] Clarke quotes Haliburton's words in several other stories in which he writes racist, incredibly offensive descriptions of his African-Nova Scotian neighbours and workers. Clarke argues that Haliburton used this racist imagery to uphold slavery even while he was a Member of the Assembly for Annapolis County up until October 1829.[218] Haliburton might have been a paternalistic friend of Rose, calling her his "Black Venus" (Rose was in her 50s and probably looking her age, worn out by hard work and single parenting, and Haliburton was likely being sarcastic in calling her Venus) but he had no appreciation of and was no friend of her African heritage.

End Notes

1. Moody, Barry p. 58
2. Walker, James W. St. G P. 33, footnote #2
3. Moody, Barry. p. 61
4. Whitfield, Harvey Amani "Slavery in English Nova Scotia, 1750-1810" p. 33
5. ibid p. 34
6. ibid p. 35
7. DeVoe, Thos. F. Genealogy of the DeVeaux Family 1885 p. 121-122
8. Muster Roll 1784 NSARM mfm no. 10163 p. 28-53
9. Charles Bruce Fergusson, *The Boundaries of Nova Scotia and Its Counties*, Halifax: Public Archives of Nova Scotia, Bulletin No. 22; 1966. Nova Scotia Archives Library, F 90 N85 Ar2b no. 22
10. Smith, T.W. used in Whitfield, Harvey Amani "Slavery in English Nova Scotia, 1750-1810" p. 24
11. Whitfield, Slavery p. 24-25
12. Annapolis Heritage Society, Rose Fortune – a "privileged character" website accessed September 20, 2018
13. Diemer, Andrew "Free Black Communities" in *Encyclopedia of Greater Philadelphia*. 2017 p. 1
14. ibid
15. Whitfield, The Struggle Over Slavery, p. 2
16. ibid
17. *The Virginia Gazette*, April 29, 1773
18. DeVoe, Thos. The Genealogy of the DeVeaux family
19. History placard, Town of Annapolis Royal, photo taken 09-09-2018
20. Whitfield, Harvey Amani "Slavery in English Nova Scotia" p. 35
21. ibid p. 28
22. Fry, Herbert, C. p. 1
23. Calnek, W.A. and Savary, A.W. "History of the County of Annapolis," Appendix to Chapter XVI , William Briggs, pub. 1897 p. 293
24. Thompson, Kent *The Man Who Said No* p. 224-225
25. Whitfield, Slavery in NS p. 33
26. Cottreau-Robins, Catherine M.A., A Loyalist Plantation in Nova Scotia 1784-1800

27. Whitfield English Nova Scotia p. 36
28. ibid p. 26
29. Mannette, J.A. 1988 p. 111
30. ibid p. 112
31. ibid
32. ibid p. 13
33. ibid
34. Walker, James W. St. G. "The Black Loyalists" p. 28
35. Mannette, J.A. p. 112
36. McConnell, Brian The Black Cemetery at Conway, Nova Scotia as a Reminder of Brinley Town and the Loyalists p. 4
37. Mannette, p. 112-113
38. Map Annapolis Website - Black Loyalists - Granville http://mapannapolis.ca/Black-loyalists/
39. Black Loyalists: Our History, Our Community http://epe.lac-bac.gc.ca/100/205/301/ic/cdc/Blackloyalists/index.htm
40. Africans in America/Part 3/Founding of Pennsylvania Abolition Society on website PBS.org
41. ibid
42. Annapolis Heritage Society website "Rose Fortune – a 'privileged character' http://annapolisheritagesociety.com/community-history/notable-personalities-past/rose-fortune-privileged-character/
43. Holmes Whitehead, Ruth. p. 26
44. Diemer, Andrew "Free Black Communities" in *Encyclopedia of Greater Philadelphia* website: http://philadelphiaencyclopedia.org/archive/free-Black-communities/
45. ibid
46. https://unknownnolonger.virginiahistory.org/record/1013/259 Image 1
47. https://unknownnolonger.virginiahistory.org/record/1013/259 Image 3
48. http://www.fortunestory.org/fortune/
49. ibid
50. Tredyffrin Easttown Historical Society; *Historical Quarterly Digital Archives*, Winter 2004, Vol.1 No.1 Pp. 3-12
51. Lewis, Danny The Smithsonian.com "The New York Slave Revolt was a Bloody Prelude to Decades of Hardship." April 6, 2016

https://www.smithsonianmag.com/smart-news/new-york-slave-revolt-1712-was-bloody-prelude-decades-hardship-180958665/

52. Soderlund, J.R. "Black Women in Colonial Pennsylvania" *The Pennsylvania Magazine of History and Biography* Vol. 107, No. 1 (Jan. 1983), p. 51

53. ibid

54. ibid p. 62

55. ibid

56. Personal Conversation, two descendants, sisters
    Personal Conversation, one descendant, male

57. ibid

58. Soderlund p. 61

59. Soderlund 1983 p. 61

60. ibid p. 63

61. ibid

62. ibid p. 64

63. ibid

64. ibid p. 65

65. ibid

66. Holmes Whitehead, Ruth 2013 p. 148

67. ibid p. 146

68. Holmes Whitehead p. 144

69. Diemer, p. 2

70. ibid p. 4

71. Northup, Solomon "Twelve Years a Slave"

72. https://Blackpast.org/aah/lord-dunmore-s-proclamation-1775

73. ibid

74. Holmes Whitehead p. 65

75. ibid p. 66

76. ibid

77. Mannette, J.A. p. 108

78. ibid p. 103

79. Morton, Suzanne p. 188

80. PANS mfm no. 10163, pp. 28-53 Muster Roll of Discharged Officers, Disbanded Soldiers and Loyalists in Annapolis County 18-24, June 1784

81. https://www.babynames.co.uk/names/aminata/ accessed Oct. 30, 2018
82. Hill, Lawrence, *The Book of Negroes*
83. Whitfield, North to Bondage, p. 43
84. ibid p. 36
85. ibid p. 43
86. Whitfield 2016 p. 71-79
87. Whitfield 2012, p. 10
88. Holmes Whitehead, Ruth, p. 126-127; see also Whitfield, H.A. 2012 p. 10
89 http://Blackloyalist.com/cdc/people/secular/postell.html Accessed Oct. 14, 2018
90. Whitfield 2009 p. 26
91. Elliott Clarke, George "White Niggers, Black Slaves: Slavery, Race and Class in T.C. Haliburton *The Clockmaker, Nova Scotia Historical Review*, Vol. 14, No. 1 1994 p. 30
92. Walker, James. St. G p. 41
93. Whitfield, 2012 p. 6
94. Moody, Barry p. 64
94. Walker, James p. 45
96. ibid
97. Moody, p. 64
98. Walker, p. 52-53
99. ibid
100. ibid p. 49
101. ibid p. 53
102. Walker, p. 53, footnote number 55 quoting David George in *Life* p. 499
103. ibid p. 41
104. ibid
105. PANS, Vol. 19 #38
106. Holmes Whitehead p. 160
107. Walker, p. 66
108. ibid
109. Diemer, Andrew p. 4
110. ibid

111. ibid
112. ibid. p. 67
113. Walker, p. 67-69 footnote number 16
114. ibid p. 68
115. http://Blackloyalist.com/cdc/people/religious/leonard.htm
     Accessed November 10, 2018
116. ibid
117. ibid
118. ibid
119. http://Blackloyalist.com/cdc/people/religious/leonard.html
     Accessed November 10, 2018
120. ibid
121. Walker p. 24-27
122. ibid p. 27
123. O'Dell Museum, Annapolis Royal mfm no. 2 Baptisms Trinity
     Anglican Church
124. Walker p. 385
125. ibid p. 27
126. ibid p. 44
127. ibid
128. ibid
129. ibid
130. ibid
131. ibid
132. ibid p. 49
133. Holmes Whitehead p. 164 quoting the journal of Boston King
134. Walker p. 95
135. ibid p. 94-95
136. ibid p.97
137. Walker, James W. St. G. p. 229-231
138. Pachai, Bridglal and Bishop, Henry p. 11
139. ibid
140. O'Dell Museum records, Trinity Anglican Church, mfm no. 2
     Reverend Roger Viets Baptisms,
141. Greenwood p. 42

142. ibid p. 11

143. ibid

144. ibid p. 39

145. O'Dell House Museum mfm #2- Burials

146. ibid

147. ibid

148. ibid Baptisms

149. Lawrence, Ian, notes in O'Dell museum in file marked "Rose Fortune"

150. Winks, Robin "The Blacks in Canada: A History" 2nd Edition p. 73, McGill Queen's Press 1997

151. Morton, Suzanne 1993 p. 188

152. Cottreau-Robins, Catherine, A Loyalist Plantation in Nova Scotia, 1784-1800

153. Perkins, Charlotte Isabella p. 88

154. ibid

155. Morton, p. 192

156. Conversation with two descendants, sisters

157. Fort Anne Scrap Books, mfm#1 Newspaper clipping from the *Sunday Leader*

158. Morton, pl. 198

159. ibid p. 200

160. Perkins, Charlotte p. 142

161. Annapolis Heritage Society website: Rose Fortune www.annapolisheritagesociety.com/community-history/notable-personalities-past/rose-fortune-privledged-character/

162. Perkins, Charlotte, p. 29

163. Morton, p. 200

164. ibid

165. Morton, p. 165

166. Lawson, Mary Jane Katzmann 1893 p. 188-190

167. Morton, p. 165

168. Mannette p. 115

169. Bull, Mary Kate p. 32

170. ibid

171. ibid

172. Whitfield, The Struggle p. 15

173. Morton. p. 203

174. ibid

175. Mannette, p. 122

176. ibid

177. ibid

178. ibid

179. ibid (quoting Walker, 1976, p. 85)

180. NSARM, RG 34-301 vol. 1, Grand Jury Book 1801-1861 April Sessions 1836, April Sessions 1839

181. The Disorderly Houses Act of 1751, Parliament of Great Britain, Section 8

182. Walker, p. 55-56

183. PANS RG (J.1) 1787-1842

184. ibid

185. NSARM, RG 34-301 vol.1, Grand Jury Book 1801-1861 April Sessions 1836, April Sessions 1839

186. PANS MG 15 Vol 20 #53-54

187. A.F. Church Map, Annapolis County 1876

188. Conversation, Denise Rice

189. Sleigh, C.M. Lieutenant-Colonel BWA "The Icy Passage" p. 22

190. ibid

191. Rice, Denise (author) genealogy unpublished

192. ibid

193. Perkins, Charlotte p. 142

194. Black Mother, Black Daughter. National Film Board film

195. https://www.trurodaily.com/living/famous-daughter-annapolis-royal-to-honour-Black-heritage-and-inspirational-daurene-lewis-195332/196.

196 Allan, Wilber, Genealogy of Rose Fortune, unpublished

197. ibid

198. https://www.capebretonpost.com/living/a-renaissance-woman-celebrating-daurene-lewis-first-female-black-mayor-with-sculpture-dedication-words-of-tribute-240445/

199. https://ableorg.ca/pdf/fortunebutler.pdf
200. https://www.canada.ca/en/parks-canada/news/2018/01/government_of_canadaannouncesnewnationalhistoricdesignations.html
201. http://vansda.ca/heritage-trail/panel-locations
202. https://www.ferries.ca/rose-fortune/
203. https://www.annapoliscountyspectator.ca/community/good-fortune-annapolis-royal-honours-its-most-famous-black-loyalist-4151/
204. http://mapannapolis.ca/Black-loyalists/
205. ibid
206. https://delapscoveblackindianpioneersociety.webs.com/
207. ibid
208. https://www.digbycourier.ca/news/local/Black-mikmaq-say-they-are-targets-of-graffiti-at-delaps-cove-35470/
209. Coward-Ruggles, Elizabeth p. 220
210. http://mapannapolis.ca/Black-loyalists
211. Allan, Wilfred, genealogy of Rose Fortune, unpublished, based on Census Canada research
212. http://radiantrootsboricuabranches.com/
213. ibid
214. ibid
215. Elliot Clarke, George p. 27
216. ibid
217. Elliot Clarke, George 1994, quoting Haliburton p. 28
218. ibid

Bibliography

Allen, Wilfred, Unpublished genealogy research of the Nova Scotia descendants of Rose Fortune

Brudenell, Edward, *Letterbook on Loyalists 1785-1786* MS CAN48 Volume 1, Houghton Library, Harvard University

Calnek, W.A., Savary, A.W., M.A. *History of the County of Annapolis* Mika Publishing Company, Belleville, Ontario 1980

Coward-Ruggles, Elizabeth, *Bridgetown Nova Scotia Its History to 1900* Mailman Publishing Co. Ltd. for Bridgetown & Area Historical Society

Diemer, Andrew, Free Black Communities in *Encyclopedia of Greater Philadelphia* on website https://philadelphiaencyclopedia.org/archive/free-black-communities/
Accessed January 1, 2019

Elliott Clarke, George "White Niggers, Black Slaves: Slavery, Race and Class in T.C. Haliburton's *The Clockmaker*" in *Nova Scotia Historical Review* Volume 14, No. 1 1994

Greenwood, Walter R. Rev. M.A., Th.D. *History of Freeport Nova Scotia 1784-1934*, October 1st, 1934, Freeport N.S.

Fry, Herbert C., *History of Devon, Pennsylvania* on website http://docplayer.net/40185358-A-history-of-devon-c-herbert-fry-since-this-land-was-not-actively-marketed-it-lay-dormant-and-was-the-last-part-of-easttown-to-be-developed.html
Accessed December 14, 2018

Holmes Whitehead, Ruth, *Black Loyalists: Southern Settlers of Nova Scotia's First Free Black Communities* Nimbus Publishing Ltd., Halifax 2013

Lawrence, Ian, Unpublished genealogy of Rose Fortune and Charles Francis

Mannette, J.A. 'Stark Remnants of Blackpast': Thinking on Gender, Ethnicity and Class in 1780s Nova Scotia, unpublished paper, 1984 from: http://www.alternateroutes.ca/index.php/ar/article/view/20281
Accessed Oct. 12, 2018

Moody, Barry, *A History of Annapolis Royal: A Town with a Memory* Nimbus Publishing, Halifax and the The Historical Association of Annapolis Royal, 2014

Morton, Suzanne, "Separate Spheres in a Separate World: African-Nova Scotian Women in Late-19th Century Halifax County" in *Separate Spheres: Women's Worlds in the 19th-Century Maritimes*, eds. Guildford, Janet & Morton, Suzanne, Acadiensis Press, Fredericton, New Brunswick, 1994

O'Dell Museum, mfm #2 Reverend Roger Viets Trinity Anglican Church Baptisms, Burials, First Communions, Marriages.

Pachai, Bridglal & Bishop, Henry, *Images of our Past: Historic Black Nova Scotia* Nimbus Publishing, Halifax, 2006

Perkins, Charlotte Isabella, *The Romance of Old Annapolis Royal*, Boulder Publications for the Historical Association of Annapolis Royal, 1988

Rice, Denise and Ritchie, Ruth, *Lequille ~ Chronicles of a Community* 2011

Rice, Denise, Unpublished genealogy of Rose Fortune

Thompson, Kent, *The Man Who Said No: Reading Jacob Bailey*, Gaspereau Press Printers & Publishers, 2008

Walker, James W. St. G. *The Black Loyalists: The Search for a Promised Land in Nova Scotia and Sierra Leone 1783-1870*

Whitfield, Harvey Amani, *North to Bondage; Loyalist Slavery in the Maritimes* UBC Press, Vancouver, 2016

———— "Slavery in English Nova Scotia, 1750-1810" in *Royal Nova Scotia Historical Society Journal*, Volume 13, 2010

————"The Struggle over Slavery in the Maritime Colonies" *Acadiensis*, Volume XLI, No. 2 Summer/Autumn

Virginia Gazette newspaper (Purdie & Dixon), Williamsburg, VA, April 29, 1773

Virginia Gazette newspaper, Williamsburg, VA, June 17, 1773

Index